CAMBRIAN WAY

CAMBRIAN WAY

Richard Sale

ISBN: 0-86381-605-3

Cover design: Alan Jones

First published in 1983 by
Constable & Co. Ltd. London.
New Edition in 2000 by
Gwasg Carreg Gwalch, 12 Iard yr Orsaf, Llanrwst, Wales LL26 0EH
☎ 01492 642031 📠 01492 641502
✆ books@carreg-gwalch.co.uk   Website: www.carreg-gwalch.co.uk

To Nathan

Contents

Introduction

Preface

The geographical structure of Wales is ideally suited to a long-distance footpath, if we accept that such paths should concentrate on high land. This suitability was recognised in the late 1960s by groups that had completed the 'construction' of what is now the Offa's Dyke National Trail, partly along the English-Welsh border. The possibility of such a route, called the Cambrian Way from an early stage, was taken up by the Countryside Commission, the official government arm for designating long-distance footpaths, and by the Cambrian Way Committee. The latter was a self-styled group representing leading countryside groups, the Ramblers' Association and the Youth Hostels Association, under the chairmanship of Tony Drake, a leading member of both organisations. Tony was largely responsible for surveying a route which the Committee presented to the Countryside Commission for consideration. This route was 'high level', covering all the main mountain blocks in south and north Wales. After it was challenged by several groups, the Commission prepared a mainly lowland alternative for discussion. The Cambrian Way Committee was unhappy with this, feeling, with justification, that it failed to live up to the promise that Wales offered the walker.

The Commission was now in a difficult position. If it continued with its proposed route it would antagonise those organisations in favour of the path, while only marginally placating the major dissenters. If, instead, it accepted the Committee's route it would antagonise those organisations opposed to the way in principle. The Commission's situation was not helped by the adverse publicity that both the Cambrian Way and other long footpaths were attracting in the walking press at that time. The Commission attempted to compromise, appointing field officers to survey all proposals in, firstly, south Wales, then, later, in mid-Wales, though never in north Wales. In

9

the event, all attempts at compromise failed, and in early 1982 the project was abandoned.

Those influenced by the SGR system of French-speaking Europe, the Wanderweg of German Europe and the efforts of the European Ramblers' Association will be saddened by the decision. Those appalled by erosion and traffic on the Pennine Way will be heartened. The truth, if truth there be, must lie between these extremes. What the decision does mean is that anyone wanting to walk the length of Wales, from Cardiff to Conwy, can now make his own decision as to his route. This book offers the author's route, one which draws on his own work over many years, independent of both Commission and Committee, though drawing on their work also, the latter as a result of several enjoyable meetings and walks with Tony Drake. It is a meandering route seeking interesting spots, scenic, mythical and historical, and exploring those aspects of the Welsh countryside.

The route follows rights of way and access – its status is considered in the Appendix on these points – but some requests and words of caution are necessary. In places it passes through isolated areas of considerable importance to the natural flora and fauna of Wales (and Britain). Almost throughout, it passes across land that constitutes personal livelihood. At all times it is imperative that the walker should consider the responsibility his presence places on him, not only in relation to the environment, but in relation to those who follow him and who will be judged by his actions. Access in Wales presents delicate problems, as do many of the scientific sites – be careful, disruption of the latter could prejudice the former.

The words of caution relate to the nature of the terrain. The route described is longer than the Pennine Way, and has twice that route's amount of climbing. If a single traverse is contemplated – and the book was not prepared with that in mind; what is described is an exploration, not a route march – it will be arduous and the walker will need to be well equipped.

The climatic section of the Appendix on Wales indicates that the decrease in temperature with altitude in upland Wales is higher than elsewhere. It also indicates that the upland areas are subject to rain and high winds which have the effect of reducing the apparent temperature by increasing convective heat losses from the body. In bad weather, parts of the route are not easy to follow; remember that there are no waymarks, and the mapping here is not intended to be definitive.

That said, it is a worthwhile route, and the walker should greatly enjoy it. To derive the greatest pleasure he should be patient, perhaps visiting some parts more than once to savour seasonal effects. To those who complete it at one go, in twelve days, in continuous rain – congratulations. But you have missed the point.

A Note on Mapping

This is *not* a conventional guidebook. While every effort has been made to keep walkers on the right track by furnishing sufficient map references, it is imperative that they possess the relevant maps. There is no waymarking on the route, which means that walkers who stray off course will have difficulty in regaining the route if they do not have their own maps. The relevant OS maps are as follows:

Maps at 1:25,000

Explorer 151 (Cardiff and Bridgend)

Explorer 152 (Newport and Pontypool)

Outdoor Leisure 13 (Brecon Beacons Eastern Area)

Outdoor Leisure 12 (Brecon Beacons Western and Central Areas)

Explorer 187 (Llandovery, Llanwrtyd Wells and Llyn Brianne)

Explorer 213 (Aberystwyth and Cwm Rheidol)

Explorer 215 (Newtown and Machynlleth)

Outdoor Leisure 23 (Snowdonia – Cadair Idris)

Outdoor Leisure 18 (Snowdonia – Harlech, Bala and Porthmadog)

11

Outdoor Leisure 17 (Snowdonia – Snowdon and Conwy Valley)
Landranger (1:50,000) series
171 (Cardiff and Newport)
161 (Abergavenny and the Black Mountains)
160 (Brecon Beacons)
147 (Elan valley and Builth Wells)
135 (Aberystwyth and Machynlleth)
124 (Dolgellau)
115 (Snowdon)
Both lists read south to north.

The Traveller in Wales

Wales has always attracted the traveller, and the writings of
those who have gone before can inspire today's wayfarer. Two
such books have been companions of the writing of this one.
First is the journey through, and description of, Wales by
Giraldus Cambrensis – Gerallt Gymro (Gerald of Wales) –
Archdeacon of Brecon in the late twelfth century. Giraldus
undertook his journey as companion to Baldwin, Archbishop of
Canterbury, who was seeking support, in 1188, for the Third
Crusade. Second is George Borrow's *Wild Wales*, a journey from
a much later time. The first is, historically, of great interest; the
second, though occasionally tedious, contains some good
insights, and includes excellent descriptive passages. That given
below could hardly be improved on as a reason for walking in
Wales:

I turned and looked at the hills I had come across. There they
stood, darkly blue, a rain cloud, like ink, hanging over their
summits. Oh, the wild hills of Wales, the land of old renown and
of wonder, the land of Arthur and Merlin!

For those who think it is a sacrilege that it is a piece of
English prose that has been chosen to describe the attraction of
upland Wales, here is the final section of a prose poem by John

Ceiriog Hughes, a Welsh poet of the mid-nineteenth century. It expresses perfectly the call of the Welsh hills for all those who must return from their journeys to, and in, them:

> Son of the mountain am I,
> far from home making my song;
> But my heart is in the mountain,
> with the heather and small birds.

A Land, a People, a Language

A Land

Wales is a small country, even in European terms, covering a little over 20,000 square kms (8,000 square miles). It is rectangular, 260kms (160 miles) north-south, 80kms (50 miles) east-west with the island of Anglesey (Ynys Môn) set off the northern coast and two western horns, the Llŷn Peninsula and old Pembrokeshire, enclosing Cardigan Bay. It is a mountainous country, lowland areas being restricted to valleys and the coastal plain, and it has produced a rugged nation.

Geologically the country is of great interest and the geology, together with its resultant geography and the effect of that geography on climate and social economics, is dealt with in Appendix 1.

A People

Britain, taken as a whole, has been inhabited for at least 250,000 years, though it is almost certain that settlement has not been continuous, since that period has seen a number of ice ages that would have forced the inhabitants southward, as well as sculpting the land we see today. There is evidence in North Wales for the existence of Neanderthal Man or, more correctly, for articles with Mousterian associations, but the best known Welsh find is later – the Red Lady of Paviland. The Red Lady was the name given to the skeletal remains uncovered from a shallow grave in the entrance of a cave in cliffs at Paviland on the Gower peninsula. The remains were discovered by William Buckland, Dean of Westminster, in the early nineteenth century. The skeleton was stained red by ochre and was wrongly sexed, being in fact that of a young man. When he was alive the site would not have been at the sea's edge, the water having encroached on the plain that originally separated it from an inland cliff containing the cave. The reason for the red colouration is not known.

Remains from the age of the Red Lady are rare, which may show that the country received only minimal settlement. By the arrival of Neolithic cultures, however, there was wide settlement, although it was grouped around the more hospitable lowlands – Môn, Ardudwy, the Morgannwg (Glamorgan) coastal plain. Neolithic folk were the first to leave an impression on the landscape, with a series of fine tombs. These can be normal long barrows, as at Tinkinswood near Cardiff or, more usually, the bare remnants of the rock slab tomb that underlay such mounds. These tombs, a capstone supported by a number of uprights, are normally called dolmens, but the Welsh word *cromlech* has been historically applied to all such monuments in Wales. The site at St Lythans, near Cardiff, is a good one, but there are many others – Pentre Ifan in Pembrokeshire being considered one of the finest. Closer to the described route, the cromlechs of Cors y Gedol and Dyffryn Ardudwy, in the Ardudwy plain between the Rhinogydd and Cardigan Bay, are also extremely interesting. In the same area are Carneddau Hengwm, a pair of cromlechs and a pair of stone circles, one of the most concentrated sites in Wales. The tombs here are a little younger, representing a link between the Neolithic culture and that of the Bronze Age that replaced it. It is with the latter age that the large number of standing stones in Wales are usually associated, although that association is occasionally based on evidence which is, at best, flimsy. The Welsh for a standing stone is *maen hir*, long stone, and it is that name, in the form of *menhir*, that has become popular in describing such stones. Lately, with the increased coverage – not all of it useful – given to astro-archaeology, menhirs have taken on a considerable significance. It is now possible to view the stones as the markers of extraterrestrial air terminals, batteries holding mystical power, or connections for large energy reservoirs. While such 'earth magic' ideas may be too fanciful, it is easy to understand the emotional tug of such stones. They stand, invariably, in dramatic sites and with the right weather conditions can represent a powerful image. The described route passes close to several, in the area around Mynydd Du, and also close to Cerrig Duon, a stone circle and alignment. No published work yet describes Cerrig Duon as a solar or lunar observatory, but the need to rationalise such sites is apparent when visiting it. It really is very intriguing why anyone should want to create such a pattern at such a site.

The replacement of the Bronze Age culture in Wales by the Iron Age peoples appears to have been by intermixing rather than annihilation. This theory rests on two bases: firstly, the finding, in Llyn Fawr, Glamorgan, of a hoard of metal objects, some of bronze, some of iron and yet, apparently, of contemporary manufacture and usage; and secondly, and more romantically, the possibility of a real folk memory behind the story of the lady of the lake that will be recounted when our journey reaches Llyn y Fan Fach. The Iron Age in Wales is deeply significant as it represents the coming of the peoples whose name is synonymous with the country – the Celts. The name does not appear to have been used by the people to describe themselves, but derives from the Roman Keltoi, which was interchangeable with Galli as the word used to describe the inhabitants of Gaul (France). The emergence of Celtic peoples would require a book in itself. For our purposes it is worthwhile noting only that proto-Celtic civilisations were of eastern and central European origin, the true iron-using Celtic cultures, firstly Hallstatt and later La Tène, being named from villages in Austria and Switzerland respectively.

To the civilised Romans and Greeks of Mediterranean Europe, the Celts were barbarians and war-like savages. By comparison, of course, these descriptions were true; inter-tribal warfare being the apparent hallmark of the Celts (and later the downfall of the Brythons), who also possessed no written language and worshipped strange (to the Roman recorders) gods. The Roman expansion into northern Europe was probably motivated as much by frequent attacks from the Celts on their border as by any expansionist dreams. The Romans were impressed by the qualities of the Celts in battle, but unimpressed by what they saw as the puerile boastings of their leaders, parading about in ornaments accompanied by men forever chanting their praises. They did not realise the true significance of what they saw. The Celts, having no literature, had invested the history of their peoples in epic poems that were remembered and delivered by bards. This had two direct results. Firstly, a heroic leader stock was created which continually broadcast their own, and their ancestors', heroism. Thus a leader who was not rich and majestic, and not celebrated in the bardic poems, was suspect and might not protect you well enough. Secondly, a love of language for its own sake developed. To such an extent was this true that the Celts actually had a god of eloquence – Ogmios. Eventually the Romans and Greeks recognised this eloquence for what it was. The Celts maintained, in essence, that the tongue was mightier than the sword and they venerated age, which increased its powers. Eventually they emerged in the classical world as teachers of rhetoric.

The Celtic tribes had invaded Britain at an early time and were long established well before the Romans came. In many parts of Wales the typical Celtic (Iron Age) hill fort can be seen. The mystical site of Dinas Emrys is on the described route, but the best site lies on Yr Eifl in the Llŷn Peninsula, to the west of Snowdon. This is Tre'r Ceiri (the Town of Giants), an immensely impressive array of fortifications and hut circles.

The Roman invasion, that of AD 43 rather than the initial, and limited sortie, of Julius Caesar, occurred for numerous reasons. It secured the northern frontier for all time, cutting out any possibilities of sea-borne surprise attacks; it conquered a land rich in minerals; and, equally importantly, it allowed the creation of a puppet state. To assist the last, the Romans played their trump card, using the inter-tribal and, often, inter-hero, disputes of the Celts to their advantage. At the time southern

17

England was effectively controlled by Cunobelinus, king of the Catuvellauni from north of the Thames, the Cymbeline of Shakespeare. According to Shakespeare, and Geoffrey of Monmouth in his *History of the Kings of Britain*, Cymbeline had two sons, Guiderius and Arviragus. Modern scholars, however, see a dispute arising between other sons, Amminius on the one hand, Caratacus and Togodumnus on the other. In AD 40 Amminius was banished from Britain and promptly sought the assistance of Rome. Cymbeline died and his warlike sons expanded their kingdom at the expense of Verica, king of the Atrebates from south of the Thames. Verica, too, fled to Rome. The Romans now had everything they needed, and they invaded. Togodumnus was killed within the first weeks of the invasion, but Caratacus (Caradog) fought fiercely and then escaped to Wales where he rallied the Silures of South Wales and the Ordovices of North Wales against the invader. He fought on until AD 51 when he was betrayed and captured. It seems that his fighting ability and his bearing after capture so impressed the Romans that he died peacefully as an honoured guest of Rome. The Romans clearly understood the Celts well enough not to relax when Caratacus was defeated, but to press on to Môn to destroy the seat of the Celtic priest class, the druids or, in Welsh, *y Derwyddon*. Much has been written on the druids, and most of that is pure conjecture as there is no drawing of a druid extant, and no contemporary Celtic literature on the sect. This means that all descriptions, except by painstaking inference, are based on the written work of the Romans, who would hardly bend over backwards to portray the enemy's mainstay in a sympathetic light. Even the name of the sect is shrouded in mystery. It could derive from 'oak-tree' since it is known that certain druidic rituals were associated with the oak, particularly the (rare) mistletoe-bearing trees; or it could derive from 'sees far', denoting the likely role of the sect as seers and magicians and, perhaps, holders of sacred information on seed sowing times or eclipses. Whatever the druids were, the

Romans destroyed them in Môn. Tacitus portrays the sad scene of the soldiers of Rome confronted by a priesthood whose only weapon was ritual cursing: the anger of Celtic deities proved no match for the short sword.

After the Roman conquest, Britain was quiet for several centuries, the local Celtic tribes becoming Romanised and the basis of the present system of roads and towns being created. When the Romans finally withdrew, however, the Brythons proved that they had learnt nothing in the occupation years and there was an immediate return to tribalism, with new kings emerging to do battle with each other. Such a system of small states with little cohesion and occasional open hostility was easy to deal with, and Anglo-Saxon invaders pushed the Brythons farther and farther west during the period between AD 400, when the Romans departed, and AD 500, when the second name synonymous with Wales occurs, for around that time King Arthur was active. The historical sources that point to the existence of Arthur are small in number and open to interpretation, yet volumes of words have been written about him. It would be pointless in this introduction to attempt to unravel the truth, or even to explore the myth – although this is touched on in the main text where appropriate. For our purposes here, it is sufficient to note that the first influx of Saxons into Britain had been requested by a Brython/Welsh king, Gwrtheyrn (Vortigern), to help him in a tribal dispute. Unfortunately the Saxons stayed and gradually pushed westward. Under Arthur, if he existed at all, then it was as a war lord rather than a king, the Saxons had been halted conclusively at the battle of Badon (near the Ridgeway in Wiltshire?) around AD 500. If there is any truth in the Arthurian stories, Arthur himself then fell victim to a tribal dispute and the Saxons were free to march again. In 577 they won the battle of Dyrham, near Bristol, cutting the country in half and banishing the Brythons to Cornwall and Wales. England and Wales had been created, and not just as geographical entities. The Saxons saw the

Brythons to the west of the Severn as the Wallas, foreigners. The root of the name is another Celtic tribe, the Velcae, known to the Saxons, though strangers to them. The root gives us Walloons in Belgium; Valais in Switzerland; the German name for Italians – Velsch; Vlachs in Romania; and Welsh in Wales. The Brythons, now isolated from their own kind, increasingly stopped referring to themselves as Brythons becoming instead 'fellow countrymen', Cymry.

It should not, however, be assumed that the population of Wales at this time was simply the remnants of Brython tribes from England, for that is not the case. The Saxon thrust had ended at the Severn and while Wales almost certainly collected refugees, it also contained the still-intact kingdoms that had existed since the departure of the Romans. The Saxon invasion had not harmed them, merely isolated them. Wales was now left in peace while the Saxons moved northward to secure a strong northern border. This was a long process and the Saxons lost interest in westward expansion. Eventually an effective demarcation line was set up between Saxon England and Wales by the construction of a boundary dyke by the Mercian king Offa. The true reason for the construction of the dyke – an earthwork which stretched 260kms (160 miles) from the north Wales coast near Prestatyn to Chepstow, is not known. Certainly it would have acted as a barrier to raiding parties; but it might also have been a frontier, that is a trading barrier and agreed boundary.

The Celtic saints were very active, roaming the country preaching and setting up small religious centres, the *llannau*. Each llan was an earthwork, or wooden, church and their existence has passed into the language, the names being passed on to the towns that grew up around the sites. Through the place names we are familiar, without always realising it, with the activities of St David (Dewi Sant), St Illtud and many others. While the saints created the village framework, the people moving out of their hill-top forts, the kingdoms of Wales were developing. The new counties of Wales have names that derive from these kingdoms: Gwynedd, Powys, Dyfed and Gwent.

Greatest of all was Gwynedd, a kingdom that possessed a mountain barrier and the fertile lowlands of Môn as a granary. While other kingdoms were important at times and their kings held great power occasionally, it is Gwynedd that is consistently at the forefront of Welsh power, and the Gwynedd kings who dominate Welsh history. In the early years of Wales as a separate entity, say from 550 onwards, the lineage of Cunedda held Gwynedd. This line included Maelgwn, the dragon, a physically immense man of apparently limitless violence, and finished with Rhodri Mawr, sometimes called the first king of all Wales. This he was not, though by his death he did control Gwynedd, Powys and most of Ceredigion. He did not, however, rule Gwent, Morgannwg, Dyfed or Brycheiniog. On his death his own kingdom was, as customary, divided between his sons and Wales lost another chance of unification in a welter of warfare. Another, later, king who is also credited with uniting Wales is Hywel Dda, who united Ceredigion and Dyfed as Deheubarth, and then took Gwynedd and Powys. But he also failed to secure Gwent, Morgannwg and Brycheiniog. Hywel is best remembered for his codification of Welsh law, a code that far outlived him. In addition to this justly renowned work, Hywel also laid down the duties of the royal household servants. The laws set standards of social care that were, in Wales, at least a millenium ahead of their time. They are still studied by law students throughout Europe.

Ultimately Wales was unified, by Gruffudd, son of Llywelyn ap Seisyllt. Gruffudd ap Llywelyn succeeded by inheritance, marriage and violence – the usual mixture – and by 1041 he controlled the whole country. Almost immediately Gruffudd over-reached himself and sought allegiances with Saxon lords near the dyke, probably in an effort to expand eastward. Earl Harold Godwinson convinced Edward the Confessor that the Welsh king represented a threat and received permission to move against him. Earl Harold invaded Wales, subduing the south and then moving north in pursuit of Gruffudd with hand-picked troops. These were not intimidated by the terrain of Gwynedd and Gruffudd was killed. Wales fragmented again and by the time the Normans arrived at the dyke, there was once more a system of small, squabbling kingdoms on its western side.

The Normans never pressed ahead with a conquest of Wales, it apparently not being part of William's plan for his new realm. Instead, he installed along the dyke, on the *march*, or boundary, of England and Wales, a line of barons, the marcher lords. These lords ruled virtually independent states, and their westward boundaries were of their own choosing. Consequently they encroached on Welsh land perpetually, gradually pushing the 'free' Welsh back towards Gwynedd. There, typically, the Welsh made a last stand for independence. Owain Gwynedd pushed the Normans back across Powys, but was defeated and forced back. Equally typically, Owain's death caused a power struggle and a weakening of Gwynedd, but his grandson Llywelyn ap Iorwerth (Llywelyn Fawr) succeeded to the kingdom in 1203 and strengthened it. He conquered Powys and, by siding with the English barons, gained rights for Wales in Magna Carta. He had successes in south Wales and when he died in 1240 the country, while not unified, had a truly independent air. It had been a considerable achievement. The lack of unity caused fragmentation, but Llywelyn's grandson Llywelyn ap Gruffudd (Llywelyn II) campaigned again for Welsh unity. He demanded, and received, the title Prince of Wales from Henry III under the Treaty of Montgomery of 1267 and the future looked as good as at any time since the Normans had arrived. Sadly Edward I was made of sterner stuff than his predecessors and invaded Wales to force a submission and homage from Llywelyn. This he received at the Treaty of Aberconwy in 1277 which reduced Llywelyn's position to that of a baron. In 1282 Llywelyn rose again, but briefly, being killed in a minor skirmish near Builth

Wells. A stone marks the spot where the last Welsh Prince of Wales fell. Llywelyn's brother Dafydd continued the struggle but was captured in 1283 and executed for treason.

Edward decided that never again should the royal house of Wales, or the Welsh, represent a threat to England. The castles of the Ring of Stone are a tangible reminder of this decision. But additionally Edward systematically removed the lineage of the Welsh royal houses by forcing the women into nunneries and preventing the men from producing heirs by long-term imprisonment or death. It was, in the main, a humane elimination, in comparison with the violence of the age. Recognising the need in the Welsh for a prince, he gave them, at Caernarfon, a prince 'who could speak no word of English'. The modern Welsh view of this affair, which is not sympathetic, disregards the fact that at the time the Welsh appreciated the gesture and were favourably impressed. To prove the point, there was comparative peace in Wales for a hundred years, a peace that was shattered only when a personal feud (and a strong desire to be rid of the yoke of England) boiled over into national rebellion. This rebellion, of Owain Glyndŵr, is dealt with more fully in the main text as several of the most important sites in his campaign for an again independent Wales are on the route. Ultimately Glyndŵr failed, leaving the country ravaged. True peace with England seemed as far away as ever but it came in dramatic style when the Welsh family of Tudor supplied England and Wales with a king in 1485 – Harri Tudur, Henry VII. Thereafter Welsh history and English history were forced to coincide politically.

Socially that was not quite so, however, with rural Wales being a poor country until very recent times. The industrialisation of north Wales, for slate, and south Wales, for coal and steel, followed the Victorian English fashion of exploitation giving the Welsh an equality with their English counterparts that they might not have recognised as such. Wales has retained much of its culture, however, as a trip to an Eisteddfod will show, and recognition of this has led, in the recent past, to an upsurge of nationalism with equality for the language as its central theme.

A Language

The language of the 'foreigners' of 'Wales' has its root, as one would expect, in the Celtic languages of continental Europe. The Celtic language that crossed from the continent was itself subject to a split, the Goidelic language group occurring in Ireland, the Isle of Man and Scotland, the Brythonic language dominating in the rest of Britain, and, therefore, yielding Welsh and Cornish. The Breton language of French Brittany is also a Brythonic language. To differentiate between the Goidelic, i.e. Gaelic, and Brythonic languages, the former is called Q Celtic, the latter P Celtic, the reason being the pronunciation of 'qu'. Q Celtic pronounces this as 'qu' or, rather, 'c', while P Celtic pronounces it 'p'. Thus, in mountain terms, Welsh has 'pen' while Gaelic has 'ceann'.

To the English eye the Welsh language is an unreadable mass of vowel-less words, with consonants back-to-back. This is, of course, not so, but based on the misconception that the alphabets of the two languages are the same. They are not the same! In fact Welsh has extra consonants, ch, dd, ff, ng, ll, rh, th being separate letters. As long as one knows one's alphabet the language is totally phonetic. A second, and radical, difference is initial mutation, the alteration of the initial consonants of words when the final sound of the preceding word is of particular form. The reason for this appears to be straightforwardly aesthetic. However the (apparently random) interchangeability of, say, fawr and mawr (large) or fach and bach (small), not to mention other worse forms, e.g. cam – gam – ngham – cham, makes the casual observer wince.

The visitor has less trouble with Welsh personal names, Christian or surnames. Indeed the lack of trouble seems to be the fact that there appear to be only a dozen surnames in the whole of Wales. The story immediately comes to mind of the

Welsh male voice choir which, in Iron Curtain days, was refused entry to an East European country because the frontier guard would not believe that there was not a decadent western plot behind a large group of men, ninety per cent of whom were called Davies! The story is told that a judge touring Wales became so appalled by the stream of plaintiffs and defendants with names such as Rhys ap Llywelyn, Taliesin ap Iorwerth etc, that he decreed that the naming system should be rationalised –

Take ten, he said, and call them Rice
Take another ten and call them Price
Now Roberts name some hundred score
And Williams name a legion more
And call, he moaned in languid tones,
Call the other thousands – Jones

It is a charming tale, and the Welsh names have a charm, one accentuated by their delight in double naming – Robert Roberts, Evan Evans, and Thomas Thomas, the redoubtable Twm Dwywaith (Tom Twice). Equally delightful is the use of the descriptive name – Williams the Milk, Jones the Post and the more comical ones, the undertaker – Dai the Death.

To attempt a comprehensive glossary of useful Welsh names would be doomed to failure. Listed below are those that will allow first-time visitors to understand the area they are traversing a little better.

Aber – confluence, but usually a river mouth
Afon – river
Allt – hill, especially if wooded
Bach, Fach, Bychan – small
Ban – peak or horn
Bedd – grave
Blaen – head of valley
Bont/Pont – bridge

Bwlch – pass
Cadair – chair
Capel – chapel
Carreg – stone
Cefn – ridge
Coch – red
Coed – wood
Craig – crag or rock
Cwm – mountain hollow, a valley with a backslope, as in the famous usage in Western Cwm below Everest.
Dinas – town/city, or hill-fort
Diolch – thank you
Du – black
Dŵr – water
Dyffryn – valley
Eglwys – church
Esgair – long ridge
Ffordd – road, pathway
Ffynnon – well, spring
Glas, Las – blue
Gors/Cors – bog
Gwyn – white
Gwynt – wind
Hafod – summer dwelling, hill-side house for summer use
Hen – old
Hendre – winter dwelling, valley house for winter use
Hir – long
Isaf – lowest
Llech – flat stone, or more commonly, slate
Llwybr Cyhoeddus – public footpath
Llwyd – grey/foamy
Llyn – lake
Maen – stone (Maen Hir – long stone or standing stone, i.e. Menhir)
Moel, Foel – bare hill

Mynydd, Fynydd – mountain
Nant – steam, brook
Ogof – cave
Pant – small hollow
Pen – peak
Pistyll – waterfall, usually a water spout
Plas – mansion
Porth – gate
Pwll – pool
Rhaeadr – waterfall
Sarn – causeway
Tref – town
Tŷ – house
Uchaf – highest
Waun – moor
Ynys – island
And remember, Dynion is for men, Merched is for ladies.

The Valleys

Caerdydd

It is fitting that a walk exploring Wales, even if only by way of its highland backbone, should start at the capital. As a capital, however, Cardiff (Caerdydd) has a very recent history, having acquired that position by royal decree as lately as 1955. As a town, Cardiff has had a long, if somewhat spasmodic, history. The area around the town, that is the coastal plain of the rivers that drain the Glamorgan upland plain – Afon Rhymni, Afon Taf and Afon Elái – has few sites dating from pre-Roman times. Between the villages of St Nicholas and St Lythans that lie about 7kms (4 miles) to the south-west of Llandaf are the remains of two Neolithic long-barrows. One of these, nearer to St Lythans, consists of a capstone supported by three uprights. The mound that once covered this burial chamber has long since shrunk to just a trace. Such structures, of which there are several in Wales, are known as *cromlechi*. St Lythans is supposed to have supernatural qualities, the capstone rising up and turning three times, once each year. The other barrow, taking its name from the nearby hamlet of Tinkinswood, is more complete and, with its dry-stone walling and hornwork near the entrance, is a clear indication of continuity with the builders of the long barrows on the Cotswolds, to the east of the Severn. The earliest settlers were gradually replaced, culturally, by the Iron Age (early Celtic) invaders from Continental Europe. The western Celts maintained a strong hold on their heritage, and by the time of the Roman invasion of Britain the difference between the Silures of South Wales and the semi-Romanised Belgic tribes of southern England was quite clear. The farther the Romans advanced from the southern coast the more difficult the task became. Having secured the Cotswolds the Romans advanced into south Wales in order to subdue the Silures. Since the Romans had invaded Britain with an eye to its economic potential as well as to secure its northern frontier, this advance into Wales was probably driven as much by its mineral wealth as the need to secure the Severn boundary, though the Silures' frequent incursions, and the potential power base of the druids in Anglesey, would have been considerations. As usual the first bases were military, including that at Cardiff, at a crossing of Afon Taf.

With the subjugation of the Silures, Cardiff became less important, particularly as the pleasant town of *Venta Silurum* (the market town of the Silures), as Caerwent was then known, was so close. Excavations in Cardiff – the original Roman fort stood on the site that the castle now occupies – shows a spasmodic occupation from about AD 70 through to the mid-fourth century. Then, briefly, the town became important once more, a more substantial fort being built to help defend the area against the sea-borne invaders from the west. Eventually, as thrusts against Rome itself increased, the Romans evacuated Britain and left the Romanised Brythons to defend themselves against the Saxons. It is likely that Cardiff was abandoned at that time, though the Welsh name Caer Daf – the fort by the Taf – indicates that there may have been intermittent use of the site. The Welsh contained the Saxon advance to the western side of the Severn for a long period aided, at some stage, by the exploits of the real Arthur. Legend has it that Cardiff was the site of embarkation of Sir Lancelot for France, and of Arthur himself in pursuit. More mundanely the area was held by descendants of Maximus, the last Roman ruler, and successfully defended after the battle of Dyrham, near Bristol, which effectively created England under Saxon rule as a separate entity from Wales under Welsh rule. A tenth-century descendant of Maximus, Morgan Mwynfawr, gave his name to the land around Cardiff (Morgannwg, the land of Morgan) which has remained to this day, and also in the Anglicised form as Glamorgan.

Cardiff was visited by William the Conqueror in 1081 as he travelled to St David's on a pilgrimage. Indeed, a Norman chronicler maintains that William founded the town at that time. It was not until the very late eleventh century however that a realistic attempt was made to subjugate the area when Robert Fitzhamon, the Norman lord of Gloucester, crossed the Severn. Fitzhamon constructed a 'motte and bailey' castle on the site of the Roman fort. As a marcher lord he was able to annexe as much land as he believed he could hold and this he duly did, installing at intervals his own knights on feudal estates. This had the advantage of protecting the main town, and Fitzhamon's own home, of Cardiff behind a Norman frontier, and sharing out the burden of defence. The defence was not always adequate and the town was attacked several times, most crucially by followers of Owain Glyndŵr in 1404.

Glyndŵr is an enigmatic character whose name is met at many points throughout Wales. Farther north our route takes us through Machynlleth where he held a parliament proclaiming his intention to promote learning by the establishment of a Welsh University, among other worthy ideas. Here at Cardiff the warrior side of the man was revealed when his army burst in through the city's west gate and laid waste to the town, firing it before departing. The scars of the attack remained for almost a century such was its ferocity.

Following the Acts of Union of 1536 and 1542, some of the privileges held by the marcher lords were removed. The effect of this was to limit the local warfare in the area. The securing of a stable Glamorgan, and indeed a stable South Wales, was of paramount importance to the English throne. The lesson of the landing of a French army at Milford Haven had been hard, but well learned. The peace that followed the Acts lasted until the whole of South Wales was caught up in Civil War. The lord of the manor at Cardiff, Philip, Earl of Pembroke, was staunchly Parliamentarian, at odds with the majority in the area. By 1645, however, particularly after the battle of Naseby, the locals were disenchanted. It was not that they had become followers of Parliament, more that they saw the inevitability of defeat. King Charles arrived at Cardiff in late July 1645 clearly expecting to

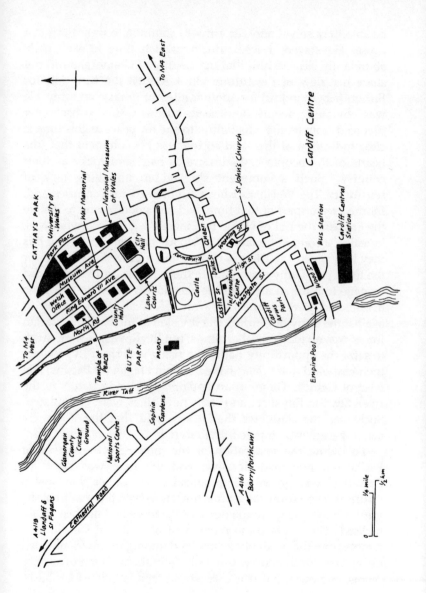

Cardiff Centre

be able to raise yet another army to continue to fight for a lost cause. He stayed a week during which time it was made abundantly clear to him that the County of Glamorgan did not share his view of the future. On 4 August the King left for Brecon (Aberhonddu) for another attempt to raise an army. He was obviously deeply depressed, but he was also becoming divorced from reality. His failure to sue for peace at this time is clear indication of this, and so too was his comment that 'the hearts of the people of Wales are as hard and rocky as their country'. Such a comment showed an appalling lack of sensitivity. The Welsh had been suppressed for centuries and, for the greater part of that time, had had good reason to dislike the English: the Act of Union had merely legitimised what was, in reality, a conquest obtained in bloody fashion. Despite all this they had joined the King in droves and followed his cause, for the most part badly equipped, to their deaths. In 1648 they did manage to raise an army, in the Second Civil War, to assist the dissatisfied Parliamentarian army of West Wales to revolt against the army of Cardiff. The division of the Parliamentarian forces was on ideological grounds, but the Royalists were quick to seize the opportunity. Sadly the rising was short-lived when their eastward march was halted at Sain Ffagan (St Fagans) just west of Cardiff. There, in an appallingly bloody battle by the river Ely, the Royalists and their new allies were annihilated. Such was the slaughter that it was said that the River Ely actually (rather than fancifully) ran red.

Following the restoration of the monarchy the power of Parliament remained decisive, and the time was right for Cardiff to emerge as a commercial town, rather than just a fortification on Afon Taf. At this time, however, the wealth of the great mining valleys to the north of the town had not been truly realised. There was some movement of coal, but Cardiff was remote from the production sites, and mining itself was not well developed. Production was mainly from the working of surface seams, and even that was carried out on a largely *ad hoc* basis.

The factors that were radically to increase the importance of Cardiff were the development of better mining techniques and the discovery of coking coal, which allowed coal to replace charcoal in the smelting of iron. Both these developments led to the construction of ironworks in the valleys to the north of the town. What the ironworks needed was a port, and the obvious choice was Cardiff. This led to the construction, in the mid-eighteenth century, of the Glamorgan canal from the Cynon valley down to Cardiff itself, and to the construction of dock facilities at the town. The impetus for the expansion of the port was the European wars of the late eighteenth and early nineteenth centuries, when the London (Woolwich) arsenal required iron in great quantities, as much as 100,000 tons being delivered annually. This increase in dockland activity also brought an increase in industrial activity.

Coincidentally there arrived in Cardiff a family which was to have a significant and lasting influence on the town – the Butes. On the industrial side the Butes constructed, at an early stage, the first docks so that larger boats could use the port, in the hope that there would be an increase in coal export. This was a relatively successful venture, but trade was still slow as it depended on coal barges on the canal. The canal was both narrow and shallow, and the competition between coal and iron barges was intense. Resolution of the problem came in 1840 with the opening of the first part of the Taff Valley Railway. It is ironic that this development, which so materially affected the wealth of Cardiff, was opposed by the canal company who had to be handsomely compensated for the loss of revenue, despite having been unable to cope with the volume of traffic in the immediate pre-railway years.

The improvement in the delivery of coal to the town (three million tons annually by 1870) required further expansion of the docks and the Butes constructed the massive East Dock, complete with the most modern coal-loading equipment. Recognition of the docks as one of the most modern in the world attracted considerable industry to the area and that, together with the finance, insurance and other commercial ventures that grow up around such heavily industrialised areas, caused a rapid expansion in population building and wealth. Again the Butes were instrumental, land to the west of their dockland complex being used for the construction of Butetown. This area was later to become famous as Tiger Bay, birthplace of many Welsh legends, some mythical, some based on real life. Now Tiger Bay has gone, as has the majority of the coal export trade that made Cardiff rich.

From a visitor's point of view, it is the magnificent civic centre of Cathays Park that marks Cardiff as a capital city, the site being capable of withstanding comparison with those of any other capital – large and airy, with an array of elegant buildings. It is surprising therefore that the site was purchased by the town from the Bute family as long ago as the turn of the century, fully half a century before the declaration of capital status. This remarkably far-sighted venture by the town deserved to succeed, and so it has – the effect of the Portland stone buildings and the wide avenues, with parkland, statues, fountains and memorials set on a site of one hundred acres being a brilliant centrepiece to the city. The City Hall itself was the first building to be opened, in 1905. The clock tower, at almost 60m (nearly 200 feet), and the fierce Welsh dragon on the dome dominate the outside of the building, while inside the Marble Hall contains a series of statues commemorating Welsh heroes. One year after completion of the City Hall the Law Courts were completed, although it was a further twenty years before the southern edge of the complex was completed by the opening of the National Museum of Wales, an imposing structure with a large dome. Inside, there is the national Art Collection containing a number of very rare items. The building also contains exhibits on the geography, geology, natural history and archaeology of Wales. The National Museum has several outlying sites, most notably that at Sain Ffagan (St Fagans, near

Llandaf), which will be mentioned later. Within the city, at Bute Street in the dock area, is the Industrial and Maritime Museum including a collection of engines and some exhibits from the early maritime history of the area.

Between the Museum and the City Hall is Museum Avenue, to the east of which lies the University College of South Wales, the largest of the colleges that constitute the University of Wales. This was opened in 1909, although it has been greatly extended since. Between the City Hall and the Law Courts is King Edward VII Avenue, to the west of which is the County Hall, opened in 1912, with a very imposing facade complete with Corinthian pillars. The rear of the building, on North Road beside Bute Park, is equally imposing. Near the county hall are the Registry of the University of Wales and the South Wales Police Headquarters, opened in 1968. Despite the inscription the building was not, in fact, opened by James Callaghan, the local MP who was at the time Home Secretary and later, of course, Prime Minster. Mr. Callaghan was prevented from attending by the crisis over the Russian invasion of Czechoslovakia, and the opening was performed by Lord Stanham. Further along the Avenue is the Temple of Peace and Health. Lord Davies of Llandinam presented the building to the people of Wales in 1938, an auspicious year in view of the purpose of the building, which was to be the centre of the Welsh campaign against war and disease. It was the first building in Britain to be so dedicated, and houses Welsh councils to the UN and other international organisations. Beyond the Temple is the University of Wales Institute of Science and Technology, a relatively new arm of the College. Opposite the Temple is the Welsh Office. Between the two Avenues is an area of quiet parkland containing the National War Memorial.

Within sight of the Civic Centre is the castle. As we have seen, the first fort was Roman. Initially this would have been a simple, and quickly erected, defensive structure, though later a more impressive fort covering eight acres was erected. This would have been a square of earth ramparts topped by a wooden fence containing the army barracks. At a later stage the walls were constructed of stone, as much as ten feet thick in places, and these form the basis of the rectangular structure we see today. The Normans repaired this basic Roman form and added the mound, or motte, and the keep that surmounts it. The mound was given a moat for further protection, and very soon after construction it was used as a prison for Robert, Duke of Normandy, captured by Henry I at Tinchebrai in 1106. Robert was held here for the last twenty-nine years of his life, the misery of his existence being increased substantially by the decision that the keep, moat and walls were insufficiently strong, and that his eyes should be put out 'for greater security'. A thirteenth-century addition was the Black Tower near the main gate which was also used as a prison, entry to a windowless, airless cell being by a trap door in the tower floor. Between the keep and the tower ran a defensive wall, dividing the castle into inner and outer wards. Much of this work is still visible, the keep being reached by crossing the moat and climbing up the steep mound. At the same time as the castle defences were increased, the town was walled completely, except for its western side which was adequately protected by Afon Taf. Some idea of the size of the medieval town can be gained by considering the position of the gates. The eastern gate was at the eastern edge of the castle wall, the west was near the junction of Duke Street and Queen Street, and the south gate was near the church of St Mary, which has also since disappeared but is commemorated in St Mary's Street.

The most striking additions to the castle were made by the third Marquis of Bute, who employed the architect William Burges to construct what is now the south-western corner of the castle. Burges added the Clock Tower, an ornate 150 feet (45m) square-sided tower, and the Bute Tower, a lower square tower topped by a roof garden, to the wall which already contained the Octagonal Tower from the mid-fifteenth century, and the

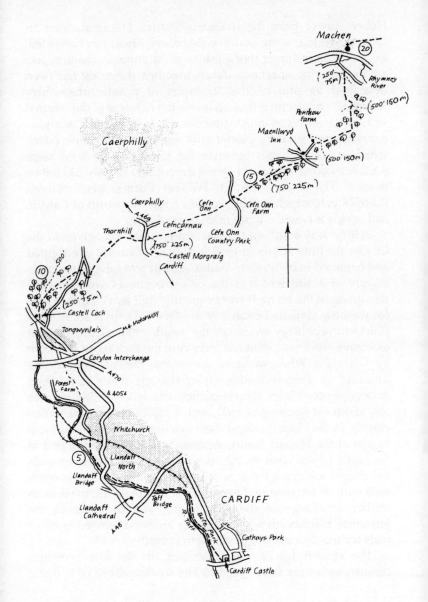

Machen

20

Rhymney River

(250' 75m)

(500' 150m)

Penrhow Farm

Maenllwyd Inn

(500' 150m)

Caerphilly

15

(750' 225m)

Caerphilly

A 469

Cefncarnau

Cefn Onn

Cefn Onn Farm

Cefn Onn Country Park

Thornhill

(750' 225m)

Castell Morgraig Cardiff

10

500'

(250' 75m)

Castell Coch

Tongwynlais

M4 Motorway

Coryton Interchange

A 470

Forest Farm

A 4054

Whitchurch

5

Llandaff North

Llandaff Bridge

Taff Bridge

Llandaff Cathedral

A 48

R. Taff

CARDIFF

Bute Park

Cathays Park

Cardiff Castle

Hubert Tower from the sixteenth century. He also added an internal western wing of domestic rooms. These can be visited, as can the Bute Tower roof gardens in the summer months, and are an amazing spectacle. Taken together, the wing has been described as one of the triumphs of nineteenth-century Romantic architecture, though it was the richness of the internal work that attracted most attention. It is a magical array of panelling and statuary, plasterwork and glass. The whole effect, which starts with peacocks on the lawn outside who seem sombre by comparison, is beyond description and should not be missed. The same architect, William Burges, also restored Castell Coch, which will be passed on the way north of Cardiff, and which is equally, if not more, remarkable.

A little way south-east of the castle, which was given to the City by the Bute family in 1948, is St John's Church, overtopped and hemmed in by modern buildings, but retaining the humble dignity of a site which is the oldest centre of worship now remaining in the town. It was originally built as a chapel of ease for the now vanished church of St Mary's. There is some early (thirteenth-century) work on the south chancel arcade, but extensive work was required following the sacking of the town by Glyndŵr. What we now see is the fifteenth-century re-building in Perpendicular style, though there have been enlargements at later stages, particularly when St Mary's was lost in the Taf flooding of 1607, and St John's became the parish church. In the Hubert chapel there is a fine Jacobean monument to two of the Hubert family, whose name is commemorated in the castle tower. Near to the door of the screen that surrounds the chapel are carved two small heads, a man and a woman, each with its tongue out. Legend has it that these are the Roman soldier in charge of the Crucifixion, and the wife of the Jerusalem blacksmith who, when her husband refused to make nails for the Crucifixion, made them herself.

The church tower was described, in the late sixteenth century, as 'a very faire steeple... The workmanship of it, being carried to a great height, and above beautified with Pinnacles, of all skilful beholders is very well liked of'. For nearly eighty years around the turn of the nineteenth century, the area beneath was used to house the town fire engine.

Cardiff Castle can be seen as a natural starting point for our route, particularly for those intending to journey all the way to the Castle of Conwy. A fine piece of walking then commences the journey, through Bute Park sandwiched between Afon Taf and the Castle. Close to here, to the south of Castle Street, and also standing alongside the river, is that monument to Welshness, the Millenium Stadium, the home of Welsh rugby. The site was named from an old inn – the Arms Park – that stood here. For such a small nation Wales has a truly remarkable record in its domination of the game, due in no small part to the fervour with which it is followed in the southern valleys. This fervour is almost religious in the crowd during matches, with massed voices singing hymns to support the home team's display.

Bute Park is one of the many parks in Cardiff, the open green areas being such a feature of the city. Farther north-east in Roath, is a 100-acre park set around a 32-acre lake. The lake has a lighthouse which commemorates the departure from Cardiff, in 1910, of Scott's ill-fated expedition to Antarctica. Over the river from Bute are the Pontcanna fields and Sophia Gardens. At the southern end of Bute Park are the remains of the priory of Blackfriars. The Franciscans also had houses in the medieval town, but there are no remains of the Greyfriars house to the east of the castle. Both houses were dissolved on a day in September 1538.

Llandaf and Sain Ffagan

Early starters may find the gates to Bute Park locked. If that is the case, follow the west bank of Afon Taf through Sophia Gardens, and cross the footbridge to regain Bute Park. Continue through the Park, following the river to reach the main A48 road. The river is a fine sight here, and, in its way, it personifies the area, rising in the uplands of Bannau Brycheiniog (the Brecon Beacons), flowing down through Merthyr Tydfil and the vale beyond, rich in memories of mining, to emerge in the eastern Glamorgan vale close to the sea. When the A48 is reached at the Taf bridge (162783), a worthwhile excursion is a visit to Llandaf Cathedral. Go up to the A48, and left (SW) where the road is crossed using the pedestrian footbridge. A little way SW, a lane leads off right to Llandaf Cathedral, visible across the playing field of the Cathedral school.

The cathedral stands on ground which has been used for Christian worship for one thousand four hundred years. It is likely that the first church here was established by the followers of St Teilo, one of the greatest of the early Welsh saints. Unusually the *llan* was not named after the teacher, but after the river. The site is also associated with two other early Welsh bishop/teachers, Dyfrig and Euddogwy, who, together with St Teilo, have caused three bishop's mitres to be part of the cathedral's coat-of-arms. St Teilo's legendary visit was around AD 560, but it is doubtful whether a true church was built at that time. Certainly there was a pre-Norman church, the sole surviving piece of which, a Celtic cross, is mounted in the south aisle. The Normans built the first cathedral on the site over a one hundred and fifty year period from the early twelfth century. Giraldus notes that the site was held in high esteem. This veneration seems to have been due to a number of miraculous events at the site – the ripening of a crop many weeks before time in order to feed the starving of the area at a time of famine; the strange death of a man at exactly the spot he had struck a pilgrim; and others. Part of this church still remains, and of particular interest is that part of the west front between the two towers, which is widely thought to be one of the masterpieces of medieval architecture. The northern tower of the west front, known as the Jasper Tower from Jasper Tudor, uncle of Henry VII, who commissioned it, was added, but thereafter the fortunes of the cathedral fell. By the late seventeenth century it was a 'sad and miserable' place, a situation in part due to Cromwell's soldiers who used the nave as a pub, and the font as a pig-trough, amongst other indignities. The sad decline was hastened by a storm in 1703 which brought down masonry from the towers, and a further storm twenty years later which brought down the south-west tower completely, together with much of the roof. Money was raised for the restoration and one of the leading architects of the day, John Wood, architect of the Georgian city of Bath, was engaged. His attempt, a classical temple rising from within the ruined walls, attached at points, but leaving some of the original un-roofed ruin, was not held in high esteem. Despite that it remained for one hundred years before being dismantled in favour of a complete restoration led by Dean Conybeare. This time there was a local architect, John Pritchard, whose work was an undoubted success. Sadly Conybeare himself did not live to see the completion of the work. His fine memorial can be seen to the south of the cathedral, outside the chapter house. Externally Pritchard's greatest work was the tower and spire on the southern side of the west front. At first glance his work, which at almost 60m (about 200 feet) overtops the medieval Jasper tower and differs in having a spire, destroys the balance of the west front. Further off, particularly from the ruin of the detached Norman belfry on the cathedral green to the south, it is seen that such is not the case, the lack of symmetry being a delight. Internally Pritchard made use of the contemporary Pre-Raphaelite artists, Rossetti producing the triptych 'The Seed of David', and Burne-Jones the porcelain panels, 'Six Days of Creation'.

Sadly, much of Pritchard's work was destroyed in 1941 when a land-mine was dropped near the cathedral, causing severe damage. Indeed only Coventry of Britain's cathedrals was more extensively damaged. Restoration work was started in 1945 and finished, finally, in 1960. To the northern side of the cathedral were added the David Chapel, a memorial chapel for the Welsh

Regiment, and the Processional Way. Most significant, however, was the addition of a large parabolic arch of reinforced concrete between the nave and the choir. The arch supports a concrete cylinder, the organ case adorned by pre-Raphaelite angels and saints, and supporting also the Sir Jacob Epstein statue 'Christ in Majesty' cast in unpolished aluminium. Again we have a departure from normality, with a clearly modern sculpture mounted on a very modern building material, set in an ancient church. It is clearly a matter of opinion, but the author finds the work and setting superb.

On the hill above the cathedral is the Old Bishop's Palace. It was the largest of several houses that originally stood around the cathedral, and is the only one to have survived. It probably dates from the fourteenth century, but is possibly earlier. A sixteenth-century record refers to it as Llandaf Castle, and such it was, the Norman bishop being a lord of the manor and, as such, able to complete a castle in the same way as other local lords. It was not in use by the time of the record, probably having been made ruinous during the Glyndŵr revolt. Entrance to the gardens, now enclosed by the walls, is by way of the original gatehouse which may have had a drawbridge, and certainly had a portcullis protected by arrow slits. Today the gardens are a peaceful place, walls that once protected those inside from marauding hordes now protecting them from the noise and cares of the real world.

A little way to the west of Llandaf in the grounds of the castle of Sain Ffagan is the Welsh Folk Museum, part of the National Museum. The castle is, in reality, an Elizabethan mansion on the site of an earlier Norman castle. Within it are a number of interesting rooms from that period through to more modern times. Outside, the formal gardens lie beside fish-ponds created by damming a small stream, and then introducing carp and bream. The formal side of the museum contains exhibitions of agricultural tools and wagons, domestic and cultural life and costume. In the parkland beyond the museum are a number of buildings that have been brought here from various parts of Wales, and rebuilt on the site as fine examples for their type.

Castell Coch

From Llandaf there is no real alternative to returning to the path beside Afon Taf at the end of Bute Park. The wayfarer could continue to Llandaf Bridge, to rejoin Afon Taf there, but this has little merit. At (144793) go diagonally right to the railway bridge. Close by is a renovated water-wheel. Now follow a section of the old Glamorgan canal, part of a nature reserve, to reach the Coryton interchange of the M4 motorway. Use a footbridge, two underpasses and another footbridge to negotiate the tangle of roads that make up the interchange, then follow the road into Tongwynlais.

The history of the iron and steel industry in South Wales will be dealt with more fully when the route reaches Blaenafon, for at that town the history is both continuous and alive in the remains that can still be visited. But it was here at Tongwynlais that the industry actually began in South Wales, the first blast furnace being constructed here by iron masters from Sussex in the last third of the sixteenth century.

Now follow the signs to Castell Coch.

Before the arrival of the M4 motorway that dominates the foreground in any distant view, Castell Coch must have been one of the most picturesque buildings in the whole of Wales. It is for all the world like a Bavarian castle awaiting the arrival of a Wagnerian hero or, as an official guide once described it, a fairy-tale castle, a back-cloth for 'Sleeping Beauty'. Interestingly, despite its apparent antiquity it is only a little over one hundred years old. The site itself is indeed an ancient one, but the present construction is the work, as at Cardiff Castle, of Lord Bute as patron and William Burges as architect. Bute's requirement was for Burges to reconstruct the original castle. To that end, the ruined original was stripped back to the foundations so that Burges could research the design concept. Among other things this showed that the original had been constructed in Old Red Sandstone, explaining the name Castell Coch – Red Castle. From the base, Burges then constructed what we see. The conical turrets he added to the completed towers were, he maintained, authentic, pointing to many medieval manuscripts that showed them. He reasoned that a flat roof was only of use if the tower held a war engine, while no roof meant danger during archer attack, for 'if . . . the arrow was fired upright, in its downward flight it might occasion the same accident to the defenders as happened to Harold at Hastings'. What he had failed to point out was that manuscripts showing the conical towers were invariably of European or Oriental origin. It is likely that all this explanation was tongue in cheek, Burges having cones because he liked them. To add to this romantic image the cones are all of different sizes and heights. The castle is entered by bridge and drawbridge through a gateway fitted with a portcullis, the mechanism for which is faithfully reproduced inside. Clearly the moat here could not hold water, but Burges' ideas on drawbridge and portcullis construction can. Within there is a tiny courtyard, not 20m across, surrounded by roofed galleries reached by staircases. The illusion of a truly medieval spectacle is lost once the visitor enters the castle rooms themselves, for here there is a combination of Victorian, Dark Age and brilliantly individual-istic decoration. The Banqueting Hall has a fine fireplace adorned with a statue of St Lucius, the legendary King of Britain in the early years of the third century. The wall murals are of episodes from the lives of martyrs.

The Drawing Room is an astonishing place. Burges maintained that he had 'ventured to indulge in a little more ornament'. He was clearly not given to understatement as there appears to be no square inch of wall surface without decoration. The decoration is thematic: the lower walls have panels representing different plants; around the doors the wildlife theme is continued, with the life-history of birds and butterflies, together with mice and snails; the walls depict scenes from Aesop's Fables; there are the zodiacal signs and figures from Greek mythology; the ceilings are birds and butterflies against a back-drop of star-lit sky. By contrast, the three heraldic shields are almost plain.

After the Drawing Room the Bedrooms appear plain and somewhat lacking in imagination, but the windlass room that contains the drive for the portcullis has interest. Here imagination is revived, Burges having provided 'sundry holes in the floor and a fireplace in order to heat water and other substances to pour down on the enemy'. Thankfully the only horde to have breached the castle's outer defences is that of the summer visitors. Externally the castle is well worth a walk-around. It is likely that despite the extravagance of the interior and the conical turrets, the castle is a reasonable replica of a small Norman castle. The first builders certainly had an eye for position, the castle being excellently sited to protect the narrow gorge of Afon Taf before it spread out into the coastal plain.

Castell Coch to Machen
From the castle the route follows the obvious track, north-east then north, through a beautiful piece of woodland to emerge on the minor road at (143840). Go right, and immediately take a lane left through trees that leads to another minor road at (145838). Go across and take the well marked and distinct bridleway to Thornhill (158845). Cross the A469 with care and go north along it to a gate on the right labelled 'Wide View'.

A little to the south from here is Castell Morgraig, a Welsh castle from the thirteenth century probably started by the lord of Senghennydd whose lands were confiscated. Because it was never finished, what remains is a true building record, the castle never having been attacked or slighted.

Beyond the gate is a bridleway across Cefn Onn, the name being given also to the country park a little below the southern ridge crest. This is another of Cardiff's wide range of parks,

Cefn Onn being a fine place in springtime when the rhododendrons bloom. The bridleway leads to Cefn Onn Farm (182856).

A little over a mile to the north-west at this point, in the Rhymni valley at the base of the escarpment, there is, at Caerffili, a town famous for its cheese and one of the largest fortified castles in Europe, a castle visible to walkers on the Way. For the visitor interested in 'real' castles, this site coming soon after the Burges works at Cardiff and Castell Coch is a blessing – the castle is functional rather than decorative. Interestingly Caerffili also owes its existence, in such a good state of repair, to the third Lord Bute.

Early work was concentrated on this site as it represented the approximate boundary between Norman ruled Glamorgan and the Wales of the Princes of Wales, but it was made redundant by the wars of Edward I. As a result of its part in several murderous royal disputes, the castle gained a black reputation recalled by a Welsh poet's wish that a dead enemy's soul 'may go to Caerffili'. The castle was briefly held by Owain Glyndŵr in the fifteenth century, but was then abandoned completely until the Civil War when it was slighted, possibly to prevent its use as a fortification, and possibly to learn more of the potential power of gunpowder on masonry. The cleaved, and leaning, south-east tower bears witness to the considerable power of the new weapon. The tower is, in fact, only 10° from the vertical, but its disjointed nature makes it appear to lean much more.

The site covers thirty acres and the castle was the first concentric design in Britain. The defences are a complex and powerful combination of water and masonry. Those who have the time should visit the site. Due to its position, a little too close to the mining valleys and too far from the sea, the castle has never really gained the reputation it deserves when compared to the famous sites of the north – Caernarfon, Conwy, Harlech, Beaumaris. It is worth a detour to measure up an impression against Tennyson's, who claimed 'It isn't a castle, it's a whole ruined town!'

Leave the farm on its southern side and follow a pathway

which is more distinct in the forest, and leads to the doorway of the Maenllwyd Inn (201866). The metalled lane to the east of the inn, running north-east, is followed. Where the lane swings left and upwards towards Penrhiw Farm, go through a gate, right, (208871) to a reach a forest road. This is followed, dog-legging at (213873), to a minor road. Turn left and follow the road to Machen.

Machen

Machen is a strange town divided into two. The lower village, now called Lower Machen though originally called Chatham after an early inhabitant, is a country village that would not appear out-of-place if it were plucked from its site and set down in any of a dozen locations in England. The church at its heart looks very English with its squat castellated tower. It was reputedly founded in the sixth century, but the present building is an amalgam of pieces from the twelfth to the fifteenth centuries. There is a sundial above the porch, and the south wall of the tower has a slab incised with a Gorgon-like face with huge staring eyes but, sadly, no inscription. This was long thought to have been brought here from a pagan altar, but it is generally agreed now that the stylised nature of the work makes it more likely to have been a decoration piece by a medieval mason. John Wesley preached here in 1741, in English, to a vast crowd who, if they gathered in the churchyard, probably upset the woonts. These were such a nuisance that the churchwarden's records of 1772 note that a payment was made of three shillings to a parishioner for 'kotching woonts'. The problem appears to have been the considerable number of woonta-tomps that the creatures (also known as moles) pushed up.

Between the villages, on the south-eastern flank of Mynydd Machen, is Castell Meredydd, built in the early thirteenth century by a descendant of Hywel Dda. It is in a very ruinous state, for after being captured by the Normans in 1236 it appears to have been abandoned and allowed to decay.

The upper village is less picturesque, although it too has a fine church set in a leafy churchyard with, at the right time of year, a noisy rookery. Special mention must be made of the spire that emerges from the roof off-centre, like a chimney. Equally interesting is the village pub which is called the Ffwrwm Ishta. Its meaning is a 'sitting bench' as compared to the 'working bench' to which the craftsmen of the village were tied to all day. What a wonderful name for a pub!

In earlier times Machen was the centre of the local flannel industry, a number of fulling mills being built along Afon Rhymni. The flannel was also dyed here, in two colours only – red or grey. The red flannel was more expensive because it was better for curing chest colds, a notion that may be more to do with some not understood herbal effect of the red dye than pure supposition. The industry did not survive the opening up of newer mills elsewhere, because Afon Rhymni had a habit of running very low in summer which meant no power for the water-wheels. This lack of continuous torrents may also explain the will of an inhabitant who granted land to the Baptist church on a lease that should be for 'as long as there remains a stone in Rhymney river'.

Risca (Rhisga)

To leave Machen, take the road opposite the Ffwrwm Ishta and, just beyond the church, take the footpath off to the right, which goes through the forest and out on to Mynydd Machen. The top is worth the visit: it is the first top on the route, an important landmark therefore, and has good views into the valleys, and of the Bristol Channel. To the north of the peak there are tracks down through the forests, but the wayfarer may also follow the road from the radio masts that is joined at (223906). The road falls quickly down through the forest to Afon Ebwy (Ebbw) and Black Vein Road in Risca.

For those exploring South Wales for the first time using the route described here, Risca is the first contact with a Welsh

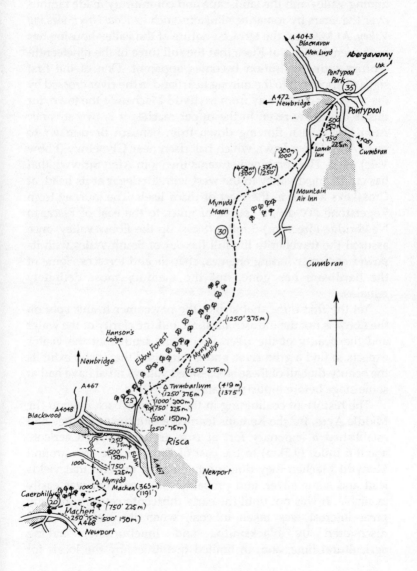

mining valley and the landscape and community made famous over the years by romantic allusions such as *How Green was my Valley*. At Machen, the terraced nature of the valley housing has been seen, but it is at Risca that the full force of the nineteenth-century industrialisation becomes apparent. One of the first signs of approach to the mining heartland is the river crossed by the wayfarer on his way from Mynydd Machen to the town, for this is the Ebbw river. In the upper reaches it is two streams; Afon Ebwy Fach flowing down from beneath Bryn-mawr to meet Afon Ebwy Fawr, which has risen near Glynebwy (Ebbw Vale) itself. The combined streams then join Afon Sirhywi, that has cut the next valley to the west with Tredegar at its head, at Crosskeys a mile to the west of Risca itself. The journey from Rogerstone (Tŷ-du), a couple of miles to the east of Risca, to Newbridge (Trecelyn) 5 miles (8km) up the Ebbw valley, once assured the traveller to the full flavour of South Wales with its power station, winding engines, chapels and terraces. Some of the hardware has gone, but the memory most definitely remains.

Yet the first thing that strikes the newcomer to this spot on the Ebbw is not the industrialisation, but the clarity of the water and the beauty of the river. It is a sad truth that the visitor expects to find a grim river, and is surprised that it still exhibits the beauty that all of these steep-sided valleys must have had at some stage before industrialisation.

The history of coalmining in the area goes back beyond the Middle Ages, for the Romans learned about the coal. They had established a legionary fort at *Isca*, as they called Caerleon, about 6 miles (9.5km) to the east of Risca. In the area around Mynydd Machen they dug for galena, the mineral that yields lead and some silver, and probably took coal that was easily available. It was not until the early thirteenth century that any great interest was taken in coal, when its usefulness was discovered by blacksmiths and limeburners, making agricultural lime, and, in limited quantities, by the locals for domestic use. The area shows many depressions left by the partial filling of bell-pits, as the earliest mines were called. Here a single vertical shaft was dug until the coal seam was hit, and the miner then worked horizontally outwards along the seam producing an excavation that resembled a handbell. Since seams that were close to the surface were at a premium, many bell-pits were dug, and the primary skill of the miner was to decide how close he could dig to the next pit before the unsupported ground above collapsed. It was a dangerous occupation, and hard work as the coal, and the miners of course, had to be brought up by means of windlasses erected over the shafts and driven by muscle-power.

Historical reviews of the valleys stress the importance of coalmining and it is difficult to realise that the coal industry was, in fact, a subsidiary industry to several others (but chiefly ironmaking) until little over a century ago. In Risca the chief industry when the town began to emerge as such was brick making. In 1747 John Wesley visited the valley on a conversion crusade and noted Risca as 'a pleasant village at the foot of the hills'. At that time it was, largely, an agriculturally based community, but the land was different in one respect from that of surrounding towns. There was little iron-stone, so important to the development of Blaenafon as we shall see later, but here was clay in abundance, clay for house bricks and clay for fire bricks. During the second quarter of the nineteenth century Risca therefore became the centre for the brick industry in South Wales. Over the course of the next hundred years, numerous extensive sites arose along the river and the canal. The canal itself was an arm of the Monmouthshire Canal that extended from Bryn-glas in Newport to Crymlyn in the Ebbw valley above Newbridge. The Darren brickworks, the first to be constructed, produced over one million bricks in the first four years of its process, and with the exception of one which was owned by the inappropriately named Fergus Brain, all the works were a resounding success. To heat their kilns, the brickwork owners used local coal. In the last two decades of the eighteenth century coal had been mined in the area by a company owned by children of Charles Phillips, the local squire. Phillips was one of the larger-than-life people that the British are renowned for producing, a giant of a man standing 6 feet 4 inches. He was famous as a hunting man and once presented twelve pairs of his own hounds to George III at Windsor.

Once while out hunting he wagered that he could jump a canal lock on horseback. Apparently he almost made it, landing head first on the far side. For his failure he not only lost his bet, but spent the rest of his life with a metal plate in his head. It appears that eight children were involved in the coalmining venture, a great number you might think, but only a small fraction of the total, as Phillips could call on twenty-six in all.

By this time the shafts to the coal seams were deeper than those of the bell-pit, and the windlass had to be replaced by a more efficient lifting machine. At the early Risca works the machine used was the whimsey. The easiest, and perhaps least scientific, way of describing the device is to say it was a hamster's exercise wheel, with the hamster replaced by a horse and a winding rope wound around the central shaft. When steam power became available, the more recognisable winding machine was used. These developments followed developments in the industry itself, which came in the first half of the nineteenth century. At that stage coal, which had been a subsidiary industry – indeed at Risca some coal production was a by-product of clay mining – became a major industry. The chief reasons were the discovery of the use of coke in iron smelting, the invention and development of the steam engine and railways, and domestic usage as fuel. Before 1840 it is estimated that a total of about 1.5 million tons of coal had been mined in the Welsh valleys. In the single year of 1874 over 16 million tons were mined. By the outbreak of war in 1914 a quarter of a million men were employed in the mines.

The history of Welsh coalmining is a story of many individuals, the most famous perhaps being David Davies of Llandinam in Trefaldwyn (Montgomeryshire), who opened up the Rhondda valley. His is the archetypal story, perhaps more myth than fact, of being down to his last half-crown when he had paid off his men for the last time. With a flamboyant gesture he gave them that as well, and they were so impressed that they worked for one last time on the shafts – and discovered the richest of the Rhondda seams. Or so the story goes.

The mines exploited by the early entrepreneurs were dangerous, with continuous high risks from water and gas. The water risk was lessened, though water remained an economic problem, by wheel-driven pumps, but gas could never be really overcome. Forced ventilation by building furnaces under 'up-shafts' – drawing clean, cooler air from 'down-shafts' through the mines – was reasonably successful, but it was the Davy lamp that finally offered some means of security. The introduction of the lamp was, initially, not a success as the light from it was poor in comparison to that from a candle, and the men preferred the candle despite the risk of igniting the firedamp. In 1860, at the Blackvein works, one hundred and forty-two men and boys were killed in a single explosion. Of the victims twenty-two were under 15, and a further twenty-four under 20. After the disaster the report in *The Times* revealed the (slowly) changing attitude of the establishment to the colliers. Before that time all such disasters were seen in purely financial, ie. owner-biased, terms. The reporter at Risca wrote, 'I am utterly at a loss to understand how any man can be got to follow a calling which, of all others by which men earn their bread, is the most disagreeable, the most laborious, and a hundred-fold more perilous. The winter will bring misery and privations to many a hearth'. The report overlooks the way in which the pits had been worked in earlier times – by fear, fear of lost wages and lost jobs. The birth of unionism in the valleys had been strongly opposed by the owners. There had been riots, often quelled by troops. In one uprising at Merthyr the commander of the troops dispersed an ugly crowd by having one of his men slice a dog in half to demonstrate his ability to handle a weapon.

Better conditions came eventually, but very slowly, and largely as the result of the increase in demand for coal. Following the First World War, however, the coal industry went into a decline and all the Risca collieries have now ceased operation. Gone too are the metal works, copper and steel, the valley having become largely silent again. The town is architecturally interesting to those who study the ribbon development of the valleys, but has a uniformity which does not have mass appeal. The church, to St Mary, was built in 1852 on the site of an older building that may even have been Norman.

St Mary's is Anglican, but in the main the religion of the town, as of the area, was, and is, Nonconformist. These chapels accompanied the workers who came to the area from rural Wales and England in the wake of the industrial expansion, maintaining faith with the people at a time when the Anglican clergy was supporting the establishment, the mine owners and ironmasters. Any visitor to Risca should therefore note the bold lines of the many chapels.

Pontypool (Pont-y-pŵl)

Black Vein Road is followed to the main road. Go right, then left up Medart Street. At the end of the street follow the footpath and canal pathway to the lane at (234915). Go north to Hanson's Lodge (236925) and through Ebbw forest to Mynydd Henllys at (248934). Here the walker has reached the terrain he came in search of, for this is very fine fell walking, even if the views are less expansive and less spectacular than those farther north. The summit of the ridge, Mynydd Maen, is as open as many that will follow, our route going above the aptly named Mountain Air Inn at (277979) to join the road near the Lamb Inn at (282991). Go round north of the inn, and follow the semi-metalled lane down into Pontypool.

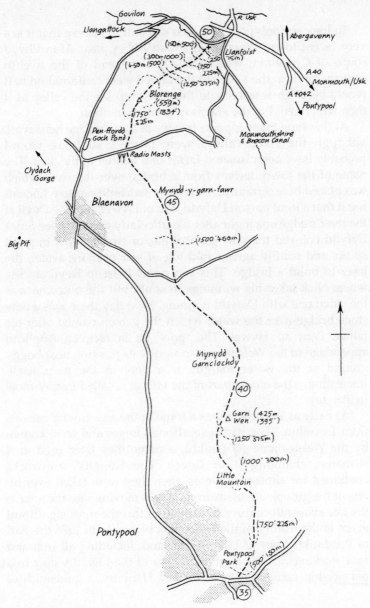

Govilon

Llangattock

R. Usk

Abergavenny

50

Llanfoist
15m

(150m 500')

(300m 1000')

(650m 1500')

250

750'
225m

(1250' 375m)

A40

Monmouth/Usk

Pontypool

A4042

Blorenge
(559m)
(1834')

1750'
535m

Pen-ffordd
Goch Pond

Monmouthshire
& Brecon Canal

Radio Masts

Clydach
Gorge

Mynydd-y-garn-fawr
(45)

Blaenavon

(1500' 460m)

Big Pit

Mynydd
Garnclochdy

(40)

Garn (425m
Wen   1395')

△

(1250' 375m)

(1000' 300m)

Little
Mountain

(750' 225m)

Pontypool

Pontypool
Park

(500' 150m)

(35)

To look at Pontypool now, it is difficult to believe that it is a very recent town. When Llantarnam Abbey, near Afon Llwyd south of Cwmbran, was founded at the end of the twelfth century, lands in the valley of the Llwyd were conferred on it. It would be of great interest to time-travel to see the valley as it then was, devoid of the effects of industrialisation.

At that time there appears to have been no village here at all, although the river valleys were farmed, so there would probably have been isolated farms or a hamlet in the area. The name of the town derives from a bridge over the river which was placed here certainly by the early sixteenth century. Legend has it that a local parson Dafydd, son of Hywel, met the Devil at the river's edge one night after a particularly good supper. Since Dafydd enjoyed the odd glass of ale, or two, he was in good spirits and readily agreed to a tug of war over the water, the loser to build a bridge. This is a novel twist to Devil stories, where Nick takes his winnings in souls, but the outcome was the usual one with Dafydd winning. Next day there was a new stone bridge over the water which the parson named after his father, Pont ap Hywel. The 'pool' is, in fact, an Anglican appendage to the Welsh pont, to signify its position near boggy ground at the water margin or a pool in the river itself. Interestingly, the oldest part of the village is called Pont-y-moel to this day.

As early as 1425 there was a forge in the area run by cousins from Trevethin. They had several small forges and were known by the Welsh name *gof* (smith), a name they later used as a surname, changing it to *Gough*. The Goughs' ironworks continued for almost 150 years, then they were taken over by one of the groups of Sussex ironmasters moving into the area in the late sixteenth century. Shortly after this the most significant event in the history of the town took place, for in 1576 the Earl of Pembroke, Lord of Usk, leased land, including all iron and coal workings, in the Pontypool area of the Llwyd valley to a partnership containing one Richard Hanbury, a goldsmith of

London. The rent was one guinea and thirty-two oxen annually, with Pembroke having the right to ask for £2 for every ox he felt unworthy. The partnership had made a very good deal, and the association of Hanbury and Pontypool was long-lasting and fruitful. The influence of Pontypool iron skills was also instrumental in North America when two brothers from the town, James and Henry Leonard, built the first forge in Bristol county, Massachusetts in 1652.

Richard Hanbury was what could best be described as a rogue. He chopped down trees he was not entitled to take and refused to pay the fines imposed on him, and he broke contracts he had with the Tintern wire-works by diverting good quality iron for private sale, 'to his own lucre and gain' as the wire-work masters so beautifully put it. For this he was summoned by the Privy Council as he was seriously jeopardising the wire-works' continued survival. It was clearly a major offence as he was told to pay £100 annually for nine years, and to deliver 15 tons of good iron immediately. This was a very large fine, but by then Hanbury was hugely rich. He used his wealth to his own, good, advantage through the prosperity of his works by buying up remaining forests when wood was becoming increasingly scarce, and by building ships to carry the iron all around Britain. By the time of his death in 1608, the works around Pontypool were of considerable importance. The works and lands that Hanbury owned passed to his nephews and through them to Major John Hanbury, a lawyer who gave up practice in order to concentrate on iron, and money, making. By the late seventeenth century the works were profitable enough to allow certain experimentation to take place. The first innovation was in 1682 when Thomas Cooke was brought down from Stonebridge, and succeeded in not only raising the general level of mechanisation but in producing the first rolling mill. The patent for this was not actually granted until 1728, for 'expanding bars by the means of compressing cylinders'. The original cylinders were operated by water-wheel, both upper and lower rollers moving to produce good quality plate in large quantities. With the plate, Hanbury made saucepans and kettles at about one-third of the cost of normal wares, cornering the market and producing considerable profits. Following the production of plate iron, experiments were carried out in the tinning of the plates using Cornish tin. By 1720 success had been achieved, and a tinplate industry was started in the town. Such was the expertise here that a tinplate works set up in Worcestershire had first to pay £36. 15s. for 'information in tinning' to the Pontypool owners.

Later again, the work of Thomas Allgood, a Northamptonshire man, employed by the Hanbury family to manage the Pont-y-moel works, led to the production of Pontypool Japan ware. Allgood discovered that varnishes extracted from coal allowed him to produce a lacquer that would give thin iron plate a very hard shell with good colour and an excellent smooth surface. The plate produced was called Japan ware because of its similarity to Japanese lacquering. Later there were many makers of Japan ware, but that from Pontypool remained the most prized, the colours being particularly brilliant, and the lacquer being heat-resistant allowing kettles to be made, as well as the standard trays and tea caddies. The actual recipe of the varnish and the lacquering technique remained a closely guarded secret. The best work produced by the local works dates from the last twenty years of the eighteenth century when the tinplate produced here was of very high quality. The background colour of the ware was invariably black, and this perfectly set off the designs among which butterflies figure strongly.

A fine feature of the town is the park at its heart. This also allows the visitor to take a traffic-free walk and see some of the better sites in the town. Just over the bridge from the car park, near the leisure centre and to the right of the path, is the site of Richard Hanbury's first forge. The remains were here until the early nineteenth century when a later member of the family removed them. Up river another bridge and pathway leads to the town's main street, Hanbury Road, near to the Town Hall, a building in the grand style from 1850, and St James' Church, a very modern building compared with the old church at Trevethin. North of the bridge is Pontypool Park House, home of the Hanbury family. The frontage dates from around 1700, but most of the house is later, building work having been carried on for about one hundred and fifty years by various members of the family. It is a fine building, but equally fine are the stables next door built in late Georgian style, with an elegant archway leading to a cobbled square. The stable block now houses a museum to the industrial history of the Llwyd valley. Opposite the stables there is a small brick-built ice store. Here ice, from the ponds in the winter and brought in by rail in summer, would be laid between layers of straw to produce a refrigerator.

Blaenafon

Returning now towards the leisure centre the wayfarer passes a shrine to the Welsh national game. This was the home ground of the legendary Pontypool front row, the threesome also providing Wales with one of its best ever front rows. The magnificence of the Arms Park stadium in Cardiff and the simplicity of this site characterise the game in Wales, at one level a game for local people to enjoy, at another a game of national pride. Exit from the park is made at a pair of elaborate gates (291006) erected in 1835 when the whole park was still in Hanbury hands. From there, take the pathway north. This pathway can also be reached by going through the park to its northern edge and exiting on the track that leaves it there. From here to Blorenge mountain the route is easy to follow, being distinct in the early stages and, though indistinct, lying on open moorland in the later stages. The ridge walk here is excellent, with fine views to the valleys and an improving view ahead. The 'real' mountains of Wales are tantalisingly close now, but though glimpses can be caught of them, the wayfarer has to wait until Blorenge is reached for the view to open up fully. A minor road is reached at (277077) which the walker can follow to Blaenafon to glimpse there, at first hand, the history of the valleys before embarking on his high-level passage through Wales. If he is eager to start he can continue directly to the WT station.

While the romance of the industrialised valleys of South Wales is, for the layman, clearly associated with the Rhondda valley and the Ebbw Vale, it is doubtful whether a single town characterises the area better than Blaenafon, both in the geographic sense and in terms of industrial archaeology. The valley town of legend clings in terraced ranks to a steep hillside, the winding gear of the pit dominating some part of the scene. Blaenafon has its winding gear, though it is some way from the town, and its terraced ranks, though the valley side is not steep. Additionally it has the bleak upland that characterised the area before the industrialisation of the valleys, and an enviable place in the history of that industrialisation.

The town is situated at the head of the valley of Afon Llwyd, and named for being in that situation. It was not set there for any reason associated with the river, but because of the existence of ironstone deposits below the moorland immediately to the north and north-west of the town. The Welsh ironstone band stretched from here to Hirwaun, some 30kms (18 miles), and yielded an ore that could have an iron content of up to forty per cent in the 'Black Band' ironstones, so called because of the distinctive colouration the high iron content gave the ore. There was an iron industry from earliest times in Wales, but this was forge-based rather than furnace-based. As has been noted, there was such a forge in Pontypool as early as 1425. By the close of the fifteenth century, blast furnaces were in operation in Sussex. By the latter half of the sixteenth century, however, the Sussex industry had been stopped by Act of Parliament. The reason for this are not clear. It has been argued that the need for charcoal to fire the furnaces – sixteen tons of wood being required to produce one ton of iron – had denuded the great forests of Southern England and in consequence the Admiralty was concerned for the ship-building industry. Since different woods were used in the two industries, this cannot be the whole story; but whatever the reason the ironmasters were in need of new sites. In south Glamorgan they found what they required. Here there were forests in plenty on the sides of valleys whose streams were powerful enough to drive water-wheels, which in turn drove bellows to produce the blast. Favourable conditions were found at a number of sites, several of which were in the valley of Afon Llwyd, which had the Blaenafon ironstone as an addition to the required wood and water. Initially the sites were in the lower valley around Pontypool where the stream was broad and strong. Ironstone and also coal were obtained at the time by 'scouring', a curious extraction process made possible by the proximity of the mineral beds to the ground surface. Initially the turf and top soil would be loosened over a patch of land, and then streams above the land would be dammed to form a lake. When sufficient water had accumulated the dam was broken and the water scoured away the top soil, leaving the mineral beds bare and ready for working. Not surprisingly this procedure has had a lasting effect on the area of moorland above the town. Originally scouring took place on six days each week. Inevitably, pieces of ironstone and coal were caught up in the scour water and carried downstream, where the old and poor of the lower valley scratched a living by collecting the ironstone and gaining some comfort from the coal each winter. Under Cromwell this practice came to the notice of the Exchequer, who promptly taxed the gatherers. The tax was short-lived, however, the valley folk deciding they would rather stop collecting than pay it.

Eventually the forest of the lower valleys were also denuded, and the outlook would have been very bleak but for the discovery, in the first half of the eighteenth century, of the use of coke as an alternative fuel for the smelting of iron. Now

Blaenafon came into its own for, on the one site, there was coal suitable for coking; there was also iron ore, building stone and water. Additionally there was limestone which was used as a flux in the furnace. In 1789 the first ironworks was built by Thomas Hill of Stafford with Benjamin Pratt of Worcestershire and Welshman Thomas Hopkins. The site is of such interest that it has now been taken into the care of the Welsh Office, and has been refurbished as a museum of the iron industry.

There were five furnaces at the site, built into the hillside so that they could be charged directly from above. Also on the site are the remains of the balance tower. Here water was piped into a box until it was heavy enough to lift a trolley loaded with pig iron from the casting floor level up to 'moor' level for transportation. At the base, the water was emptied and the water box was lifted back to the tower top by the weight of the descending pig trolley. Near the ironworks themselves is a small square that once housed some of the workers. One side of the square is open on to the site itself. The two parallel sides contain the two-up, two-down cottages of craftsmen and their families, while the back row was the works offices on the ground floor, and a dormitory for labourers above. The houses have also been partially restored. It is difficult to believe that in one of these tiny cottages one man, or more specifically his wife, raised nineteen children. Clearly the workers of the day, the late eighteenth to early nineteenth centuries, did not enjoy a quality lifestyle. Since the square also contained the only Blaenafon shop at the time, and that run by the company, neither did they enjoy much quantity. The obvious difference between the ironmasters and the workers, as exemplified for instance by the difference between the houses near the ironworks and Tŷ Mawr, built at an early point by Thomas Hill, lead to considerable anger. The men were forbidden to join a union, but an employers' association existed to ensure that profits were maximised and wages minimised. It is, perhaps, worth noting here that the slang word 'screw' for a prison warder originated at this time. It was not only an offence for a man to join a union but also to strike, the latter being punishable by three months' hard labour at the Usk prison, where the prisoners enjoyed the hard boredom of the treadmill. The 'screw' was the warder who tightened up the screw on the treadmill shaft to increase the labour required. With iron in demand during the Napoleonic wars, the grievances of the men simmered, but following the end of the war in 1815 there was an iron slump and wages were cut savagely to keep profits up. The men revolted and 10,000 from Merthyr, Tredegar and Blaenafon went on strike with the slogan 'Bread or Blood', a true sign of despair. Troops were called in, but the ironmasters gave in and wages were restored. The peace was short-lived, however, and for two decades trouble flared intermittently and violently. The history of non-conformity in South Wales was fostered at this time, with the non-conformist ministers keeping faith with their flock while the church ministers, especially the Revd William Powell of Abergavenny, tended to side with the ironmasters. Powell was a magistrate as well as a rector, and in that capacity called in troops on occasion to put down strikes and riots, as well as planting spies among the men to obtain a little prior knowledge. He was also enthusiastic that the troops should be under the control of the magistrates fearing, rightly, that the officers were more sympathetic to the men's cause.

Perhaps to respond to the influence of the non-conformists, the ironmasters, Hill and Hopkins, built St Peter's Church in 1805. It is a simple local stone structure with a considerable quantity of cast iron work that makes it most interesting. Window frames and sills, and tomb covers are of iron, as is the font, a feature which is unique. In addition to the church the ironmasters did raise some public buildings. Most notable is the now-closed St Peter's School built as a memorial to Samuel Hopkins, the son of Thomas, by his sister Sarah in 1815. The barely legible Latin inscription, when translated, notes that the school carried into effect 'the benevolent intentions of her deeply lamented and most deserving brother towards his Blaenavonians'.

In 1860 a new works was opened on the other side of Afon Llwyd. The stage was then set for the revolution in metal making that was to take place in Blaenafon. In 1856 the work of Bessemer and Siemens had allowed steel to replace iron as the primary constructional metal. However the processes could only produce good quality steel, that is metal not susceptible to brittle fracture, from low phosphorus ores which constituted only ten per cent of all known deposits. The problem of how to remove phosphorus from normal ores was unsolved, and apparently insoluble for twenty years, until experiments at Blaenafon showed the way. The experiments were carried out by Sidney Gilchrist Thomas, not a chemist or even someone employed at Blaenafon. He was, in fact, a clerk at the Metropolitan Police Courts, a situation forced upon him by the need to be a wage-earner following the early, and sudden, death of his father. Thomas was a keen amateur chemist and was obsessed by the problem of phosphoric steels. His early work was carried out in his rooms where he built a small furnace, but this was not successful and he once set the rooms alight. The turning point came in 1876 when his cousin, Percy Gilchrist, was appointed Chemist at Blaenafon. From then on, Thomas lived a hectic life, travelling to Blaenafon at the weekends to carry out experiments at the plant. The company manager, when he discovered the, initially, clandestine operations, was enthusiastic and by 1878 Thomas and his cousin had achieved the breakthrough. The essence of the solution to the problem that Thomas had devised was the use of a basic (in the chemical sense) rather than a siliceous furnace lining, producing a basic slag rather than an acid slag. Not only had Thomas solved the problem, but he realised that the resulting slag, rich in phosphorus, would be extremely valuable in agriculture as a fertiliser.

Following the announcement in 1879 of the discovery,

Thomas was feted in all the steelmaking countries of the world and travelled extensively to secure patents, and to meet ironmasters. Andrew Carnegie, the famous Scottish-American industrialist, became his friend and invited him to America. He was obviously very impressed with the discovery declaring, 'These two young men, Thomas and Gilchrist of Blaenafon, did more for Britain's greatness than all the Kings and Queens put together. Moses struck the rock and brought forth water. They struck the useless phosphoric ore and transformed it into steel – a far greater miracle'. He was particularly impressed with Thomas maintaining, 'He had only to appear and we bowed before his power'. Sadly, however, the hectic pre-discovery life involving endless travelling, poor diet and little sleep took its toll on Thomas and he became very ill. Despite this he continued to travel and meet ironmasters, growing weaker with every journey. Finally, in 1885, at the young age of 35 he died in Paris. In Britain Thomas never received the recognition he deserved. Abroad the best steels are Thomas steels, and the agricultural slag is known as Thomas slag. There is some evidence of change now and, most fittingly, a fine memorial has been raised at the site of the second ironworks, to the east of Afon Llwyd, where the cousins carried out their tests. The industrial estate on reclaimed land on the outskirts of the town also bears the names of the two men.

In the wake of the discovery a new company was formed at Blaenafon, but the difficulty in obtaining ore meant that steel production finally stopped in the town in 1938. More recently the site of the new ironworks has been taken over by a new metal-working company producing and working special alloys, chiefly for the aerospace industries.

The most tangible reminder of the Blaenafon steel industry is the Workmen's Hall and Institute. This was opened in 1894 with steelworkers and miners paying weekly contributions to pay off mortgages taken on their houses by some of the founders. Many such buildings were raised in the valleys at that time, but this at

Blaenafon is, arguably, the finest one ever built. At the outset it was decided that the buildings should house a library, paid for and maintained by the community for half a century, until the County Council took it over. The building is a tribute to the men who built it.

From earliest times, and particularly after the discovery of iron smelting by coke fuel, Blaenafon had a coal industry. In 1840 when a Parliamentary commission was set up to investigate conditions in mines they visited Blaenafon, and what they found there led directly to the Mines Act of 1842. In the pits they found women stripped to the waist hauling coal trams, and young children performing critical functions underground for many hours alone each day. This use of children often led to appalling accidents when they were left in charge of machinery, on occasions even the winding gear. The Commission found a boy of seven already a veteran of three years in the mine, who smoked a pipe all day in order to stay awake, and a girl not quite seven who was asleep in pitch darkness. Her lamp had gone out and the rats had eaten her lunch and so she had gone to sleep alone in the dark. She was lucky, she had been in the pit only fifteen months. The Commission reported to Parliament noting that in 1838, the latest year when complete records were available, there had been, throughout British mines, fifty-eight deaths of children under thirteen, and sixty-two more of children from thirteen to eighteen. Now, 150 years removed from the Commission's report, it is obvious to us that the whole of Parliament would be appalled by these facts. It was not, some members claiming that to ban children from the mines would bring about the collapse of the industry.

Nevertheless the Mines Act was passed forbidding women and girls, and boys under ten, to work underground. It was opposed by both the families, who needed the money, and the mine owners, who wanted the higher profits available from using cheaper labour. In consequence the law was ignored, and inspectors of mines were appointed in 1850 to ensure compliance. The first inspector at Blaenafon turned out seventy women and children, and was promptly besieged by the women angry at their loss of income. It took several years for the practice to die completely.

The last working pit in Blaenafon, Big Pit to the north-east of the town, closed only in the 1970s. It was one of the oldest shaft pits in South Wales with galleries dating from the very early nineteenth century. Immediately it was closed it was taken over for refurbishment as a mining museum, with tours of both the above-ground buildings and the underground workings.

Little remains on the moorland to the north-east of Blaenafon as a memorial to the town's industrial past, a situation very different from that which exists to the north-west of the town where a jumble of open-cast mines and scourings now even obliterate the route taken by the tramway down to the works. To the west of the radio masts, however, the Penfforddgoch Pond is a reminder of the industrial past. The pond is not natural, though the years have softened the artificial edges and given it a 'real' look. It was constructed to supply the forge at Garnddyrys a little way north, and down the hill.

Blaenafon to Abergavenny (Y Fenni)

Whether the wayfarer has gone directly to the WT station, or gone via Blaenafon, he will now be opposite the Foxhunter car park. The car park takes its name from the show-jumper Foxhunter who is buried among the rocks at its northern end. The horse was owned by Col Harry Llewellyn of Gofilon and a memorial plaque, also set among the rocks, recalls the horse and rider's fine achievements, which included a gold medal at the Helsinki Olympic Games of 1952.

From the car park the choice of route is governed by questions of right of way and by personal preference. Those wishing to avoid the suggested horseshoe route on the Black Mountains can go westward past Penfforddgoch Pond and across the lunar landscape to the top of the Clydach gorge at (216123) from where steps descend the gorge. The A465 is negotiated by subway to the minor road for Blackrock. Go right through the quarry to arrive on the Llangatwg escarpment road at (218130), and follow it to the kilns at Darren Cilau (205153). Since, as mentioned below, the traverse of Mynydd Llangynidr is not on a right of way, some may prefer to descend to the Brecon and Monmouthshire canal and to follow its towpath to Llangynidr. This route will be mentioned more fully below.

The view from Blorenge (Y Blorens) summit is quite superb, with the Usk (Wysg) valley below, and a backdrop of the Black Mountains and Sugar Loaf. The descent is made north-east to Little Pen-y-graig cottage at (282127) from where a steeply descending path goes under the canal to Llanfoist (Llan-ffwyst).

The canal is now called the Brecon and Monmouthshire though when constructed it was the Brecon and Abergavenny, the Monmouthshire then being a separate canal. These canals were built in what can be termed the golden age of canal construction, the last decade of the eighteenth century. The era of canals was short, as the arrival of the railways curtailed building in the first half of the nineteenth century, but intensive.

In contrast to the majority of canals, the Brecon and Abergavenny was primarily non-industrial, having been built to carry coal to Brecon and to carry lime to the farmers, and other farm produce back to the markets. As with all other canals it required a company to raise capital for its construction, to survey the route and to arrive at agreements with landowners, and it required an Act of Parliament to allow construction. The proposed canal was thirty-three miles long, from Brecon to the already approved Monmouthshire canal at Pont-y-moel near Pontypool. The Act received Royal assent in 1793 and work began the following year. The Act enabled the canal company to build tram-roads up to eight miles distant from the canal itself, this concession being termed the 'mileage' in all canal costs, and this was of great value to the companies as it allowed them to offer a service to many industries along its route. The normal method of business was for the canal company to construct the tram-road and buy the rolling stock, and then to levy the company for its use. Any private owner of a tram could also use the road, upon payment of a fee, though this offer was infrequently taken up as the cost of vehicles was high. The tram-way concession explains why early construction concentrated on tram-way construction, the canal itself being started only in 1797. Probably because of the lack of significant waterside industries the canal company ran into financial difficulties which several times halted construction, and it was not until 1812 that the canal was finally completed. Though this was considered at the time to be a long time, and does appear excessive, fifteen years for thirty-three miles, it has to be remembered that the canal was hand dug by 'navvies', the short form of navigators as the men were called who dug these navigations. Their only mechanical devices were the pickaxe, the shovel and the wheelbarrow. There was also a significant amount of engineering, bridges and aqueducts. The latter were largely the work of Thomas Dadford who also did the original survey. He was a brilliant canal engineer whose route was so good that the canal required only six locks in its whole length, and five of those were in the half-mile section of waterway around Llangynidr, four miles to the west of Crickhowell.

Except for those going westward from Blorenge to cross the Clydach gorge and climb straight up on to Mynydd Llangatwg, all wayfarers will see the canal, as those embarking on the Black Mountains horseshoe go under it at Llanfoist. At Llanfoist the canal user was about halfway between Brecon and Newport. Here the tramway from the forge on Blorenge ended, and the wharf for its barges can still be seen. There were also lime kilns here for agricultural lime, though landslips have demolished much of the original work. In the village itself the visitor will notice, just opposite the inn for instance, the old track of the Llanfihangel tramway. This was constructed by Hugh Powell, the owner of the Court at Llanfihangel Crucorney a few miles north of Abergavenny, largely for his own benefit. The gauge used was 3'6" (just over a metre), larger than normal, and this choice proved far-sighted as the line was eventually taken over by local railway companies who pushed it through to Hereford and Merthyr Tydfil. It was finally axed in the Beeching cuts of the mid-1960s.

Llanfoist was also the birthplace of Capt. Thomas James, variously known as Capt. James of Bristol, Abergavenny or Blaenafon. Despite the additions to his name he was born in the village in the late sixteenth century. In his early twenties he sailed, in 1612, with an expedition to find the North-West Passage. The previous year Henry Hudson had discovered Hudson Bay while attempting to do the same thing, but had later been cast adrift with his fourteen-year old son and several loyal members of the crew when the remainder of his crew mutinied. Hudson and his party were never seen again. It seems that the young James was very impressed by this cautionary tale and when he was forming his own crews in later life he chose only those men who were 'unmarried, approved able and healthy seaman, privately recommended for their ability and faithfulness'. Following his early brush with northern Canada his life sinks into obscurity, but in 1631 the merchants of Bristol petitioned King Charles I to approve him as leader of an expedition to find the North-West Passage in competition with a London-backed expedition led by Luke Foxe. James was duly approved, and sailed in May of that year in a ship named after Charles' Queen, the *Henrietta Maria*, Foxe captaining the *Charles*. An interesting sidelight on attitudes in seventeenth century (and later!) England is cast by the fact that the two captains carried identical personal letters to the Emperor of Japan. The letters were in English as it was believed that the Emperor, as a cultured man, would obviously speak it. James' ship reached Greenland in June and Hudson Bay in July, but conditions were very bad. James explored the southern area of Hudson Bay,

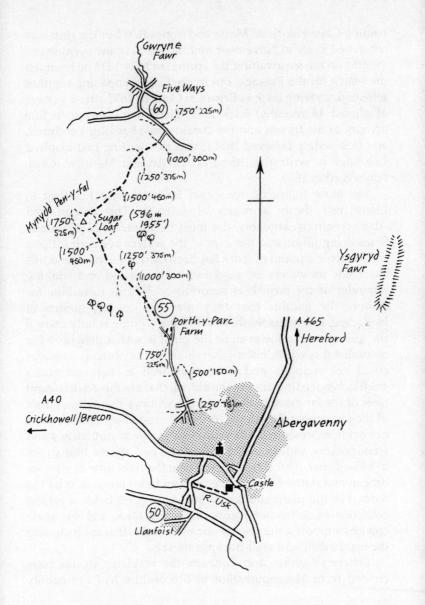

naming Cape Henrietta Maria and James Bay, but the ship was entombed in ice in November and he and his crew spent seven months on the ice awaiting the spring. In May 1632 he resumed the search for the Passage, but in the face of appalling weather retreated, arriving back in Bristol in October 1632 after a voyage of almost 18 months. Back in England James wrote a fine account of the travels and the considerable hardships endured, and it is widely believed that it was this writing that inspired Coleridge to write the 'Rime of the Ancient Mariner'. Capt. James died in 1635.

For those following the canal towpath from Llanfoist to Llangynidr there is much of interest. The Brecon and Abergavenny is, arguably, the most beautiful canal in Britain. Since being taken into the care of the waterways authorities a considerable amount of work has been carried out on it, and this has made its waters an asset rather than a sad and stinking reminder of the past. It is notoriously difficult to outline for visitors the wildlife that they may see on any stretch of landscape, as invariably that part of the wildlife is only there if the visitor is not. However, as the canal is such a delight to the naturalist it is worth noting that quiet and unobtrusive visitors could see redpolls and siskins as well as the commoner goldfinches feeding among the alders, that are the predominant trees of the far canal bank. There are willows that house all six of the commoner British tits, only the crested and bearded tits not being represented. There are tree creepers, nuthatches and woodpeckers, and above the water itself perhaps the blue streak of a kingfisher. Also above the water at the right time of year are dragon and damsel flies, while on it and in it are insects by the score. For the plant enthusiast the water itself holds a typical collection of still-water plants, including lilies, and the stone crevices support a number of our more delicate ferns including the maidenhair and wall-rue spleenworts.

Between Gofilon and Gilwern the wayfarer would have crossed from Monmouthshire to Breconshire had not county boundaries been redrawn. Now he has to make three more kilometres westwards before crossing into Powys.

Near the canal in the section from Llangatwg to Talybont can occasionally be found the dwarf elder, known in Welsh as Ysgawen Fair, but here as Llysiau Gwaed Gwŷr, the herb of the blood of men, from a belief that it could grow only in earth soaked in the blood of Danes killed in battle. Battles with the Danes were fought in the Usk valley during their incursions into Wales.

The canal tow-path is left at Cwm Crawnon (144198) beyond Llangynidr village in favour of the minor road heading south-west towards the Beacons. This is followed until a pathway branches off to the right at (133191). This leads to Bwlch-y-waun (116189) and on to a metalled, though hardly drivable road (110188). This is followed south, but at (102177) is left in favour of the pathway going down to the road at (081174). Turn left and follow the road to (049168) where a drivable track leads off right to the Neuadd reservoirs, and the suggested route.

From Llanfoist the suggested route continues by roadway to Abergavenny. An alternative is to take the footpath going east along the northern bank of the Usk, branching off left at the obvious break to move directly towards the castle. In view of the history of both town and castle this is an excellent approach, and the river bank here offers a good walk.

The Brecon Beacons National Park

Abergavenny (Y Fenni)

Abergavenny is immediately of interest to those who have but a passing interest in the Welsh language and who, as a result, believe that the prefix 'Aber . . . ' is used only for towns at the mouths of rivers. Indeed, so often is the prefix used in this way that it can come as a surprise to learn that the word does not mean 'mouth', but rather, 'confluence'. It is true that the confluence normally referred to is that of a river and the sea, but here it is river and river, with Afon Gafenni joining the Usk (Afon Wysg).

At this point the Usk is emerging from a fairly tight valley with high peaks on each side, the Brecon Beacons and the Black Mountains. After Abergavenny (Y Fenni) it flows in more open land on its journey towards the sea. The town is beautifully situated at the end of the valley. To the south is the mass of Blorenge (Blorens), and to the north-west is Sugar Loaf (Mynydd Pen-y-fâl). To the north-east is Skirrid, the Anglicised name of Ysgyryd Fawr. This is an elliptical peak with a deep cleft at one end. The cleft was actually formed by a landslip, but one ancient legend maintains it was split at the time of the Crucifixion. Another legend claims that the land sank below the weight of Noah's Ark when it came to rest. For either of these two reasons the mountain was held to be sacred, and a chapel was built (to St Michael) on its summit. This was abandoned long ago and now only a windswept ruin remains on this, the Holy Mountain.

Inevitably the Romans, those masters of the art of war, realised the importance of holding the valley-mouth at this junction of streams. They built a fort here, naming the site *Gobannium* from the minor stream. It was probably not lost on the Romans that the stream was itself named from the Welsh (Brythonic) name for a blacksmith, because of the iron smelting that was carried out in the area.

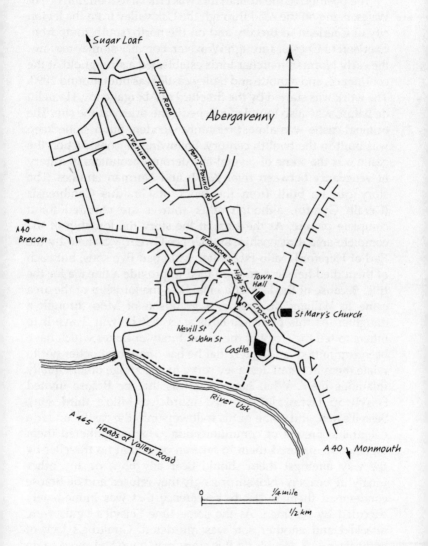

Abergavenny

↑ Sugar Loaf

Hill Road

Avenue Rd

Pen-y-Pound Rd

← A40 Brecon

Frogmore St

High St

Town Hall

Cross St

St Mary's Church

Nevill St

St John St

Castle

River Usk

A 465 Heads of Valley Road

A 40 ↓ Monmouth

0   ¼ mile
     ½ km

The position of the Roman fort was crucial to their defence of Wales, being on the road through the Usk valley from the legion city of Caerleon to Brecon, and on the north/south route from Caerleon to Chester through Wroxeter. For very similar reasons, the early Norman marcher lords established a stronghold at the confluence, and a motte and bailey castle was built around 1090. The work was started by the first lord of Abergavenny, Hamelin de Balun, who also founded a Benedictine priory at the site. The original castle was almost certainly wooden, but a stone keep was built in the twelfth century. Following its construction the castle was the scene of several murderous encounters in a story of vengeance between rival Welsh and Norman families. The story can be built from the work of Giraldus Cambrensis (Gerallt Gymro), although other sources are required for a complete picture. At the start of the story the lordship of the complete area, Breconshire and Upper Gwent, was held by the Earl of Hereford, Milo Fitzwalter. Milo had five sons, but each of them died heir-less and so failed to provide a lineage for the title. Because of the lack of a male heir, the lordship of the area came to William de Braose, a grandson of Milo through a daughter. At this point Giraldus says that he will 'leave it to others to tell the story of the bloodthirsty outrages which have been committed' and, later, that he has 'thought it better not to relate them in detail, lest they serve to encourage other equally infamous men'. What happened was that de Braose invited Seisyll ap Dyfnwal (who had murdered Milo's third son), Seisyll's son, and some of his followers into the castle 'under a colourable pretext of communication'. Having gathered them together, he ordered them to take an oath 'that no traveller by the way amongst them should bear any bow, or any other unlawful weapon'. Not surprisingly they refused and de Braose condemned them to death, a sentence that was immediately executed by his men. At the same time Seisyll's lands were attacked and another son was murdered. Giraldus's lack of enthusiasm for describing this story may have had more to do with the fact that de Braose was a Norman than any real fear that he might incite murder, for he reports in great detail the attack by Welsh kinsmen of Seisyll seven years later, when the castle was captured and burnt down. There can be little doubt that Giraldus was protecting de Braose, the unspecified events being blamed on anyone rather than him. This is difficult to understand until we remember that Giraldus was Archdeacon of Brecon and lived at Llan-ddew, only a mile from Brecon castle, and that de Braose held Brecon castle. Giraldus wrote three versions of his Welsh journey. In the first he was very hard on de Braose, but the second shows him in a different light and notes his piety. The third was completed after de Braose's death and Giraldus returns to his critical view. It is not difficult to guess at the reasons for the changes of heart. It seems certain that de Braose was an unpleasant man: confusion surrounds his death, but it is likely that following a quarrel with King John he fled, or was exiled, to France. His wife and son were imprisoned against his return to face the King, but he failed to return, his family dying of starvation.

Giraldus also recounts with awe an incident during the Welsh attack on the castle. When two of the defenders were retreating to the castle over a bridge, they were shot at by Welsh bowmen. The arrows missed the men, but hit the door to which they were hurrying, splitting it despite its being 'as thick as a man's palm'. He also reports a story by William de Braose which again testifies to the power of the longbow. In this, a mounted Norman was hit in the leg by an arrow that pierced his leather tunic, his outer iron 'cuish' (or leg protector), his leg, his inner cuish, his saddle and finally his horse, killing the horse instantly. As Giraldus says 'it is difficult to see what more you could do, even if you had a ballista'. He also notes that the Welsh bow was made, not of yew, but of elm. It is of little surprise that the English kings later took full advantage of the Welsh bowmen's prowess in their battles in France.

Following the acts of vengeance the castle remained quiet,

escaping major damage during the Glyndŵr rebellion when the town was burnt, but was largely destroyed by a Parliamentarian army in the Civil War. Now it is a somewhat formless ruin, sharing its site with a more modern lodge and the local museum.

In addition to the castle, the town was walled, and a walk around that part of it that lay within the walls is very rewarding. From the castle, go along Castle Street, to the left of which is a row of very fine cottages, gabled and with dormer windows. Beyond the cottages is a barn made of the Old Red Sandstone that gives the mountains of the Brecon Beacons National Park, that lie north and west of the town, such a distinctive appearance. Turn right into Nevill Street where, to the left near the King's Arms, is one of the few remaining sections of the old wall. Farther down Nevill Street there are several fine Georgian houses, one with a particularly good Adam-style doorway and, opposite these, a house with a row of carved cow's heads below the eaves. This was the Cow Inn of the old town. Going right into St John's Lane and right again into St John's Street, the visitor reaches the very heart of old Abergavenny. These narrow streets, that would have been cobbled originally, still show the occasional Tudor doorway, and are a reminder of the time when Abergavenny was a flourishing market town on the border between England and Wales. The streets are named from St John's Church, the original parish church when St Mary's was the priory church. Now only the tower of St John's remains, incorporated into a school named after Henry VIII who, by his Acts of Parliament, caused the Dissolution of the Monasteries and released the priory church to the town. Turning left at the end of St John's Street and then left again, the walker enters Flannel Street. This name recalls that the town was once a famous centre for the manufacture of Welsh flannel. It was also famous in the late seventeenth century for the manufacture of periwigs, the full wigs worn by the gentlemen of the day. They were made from, of all things, goat's hair. Opposite Flannel

Street is Market Street, with a very fine row of buildings which have overhangs supported on wooden pillars above a raised pavement. At the corner of Market Street and Cross Street is the old covered, or butter, market which has a very good tower. Next to it is the King's Head with an old packhorse archway leading to a courtyard. Farther down Cross Street is the Angel Inn, which has a Georgian porch built over what was a courtyard arch. With the advent of the stagecoach Abergavenny, because of its position in the Usk valley, became a coaching centre with several inns for overnight stops.

St Mary's Church is a section of the original Benedictine Priory, and a look at the exterior reveals the half-arches and closed doorways that are all that remain, apart from the name Monk Street, of the rest of the monastery. Little of the church dates from the time of the monastery as it has been rebuilt and restored several times. If the outside is a little less than exciting, the same is not true of the inside, for here are some of the finest effigies in Wales. The oldest is of Eva de Braose, a relative of William, who died in 1264. It should be noted that this attribution has been disputed, though the age, some 700 years, is not in doubt. The effigy, and that of Eva de Canteloupe, are smaller than life-size, but the fine figure of George de Canteloupe – the grandson and son respectively of the two Evas – is true scale. It now lies on a trestle table in the church's central aisle. Canteloupe died in 1273, this superb carving being over 700 years old. In its original form it would have been painted, but all traces of colour are now gone.

Pride of place must go to the stone memorial for Sir William ap Thomas and Gwladys his wife from the mid-fifteenth century, which has excellent effigies lying on a table-top tomb with some fine and very intricate carving around the sides. It is a considerable work of art. Another is the Jesse tree carved from a ten-foot length of solid oak. The tree had a dual purpose, as a sculpture in its own right – perhaps forming part of a reredos screen – and as a genealogical tree, Jesse being father of David and, therefore, head of the Old Testament dynasty. Now, sadly, only the tree-roots remain, held in the left hand. As long ago as 1587 it was said: 'In this church was a most famous work in manner of a geneologie of kings, called the roote of Jesse, which worke is defaced and pulled down in peeces'. It is still a fine work. Note especially the angel holding a pillow to Jesse's head, and the old man's fatherly beard.

Abergavenny to Partrishow

To reach the Black Mountains from Abergavenny it is best to go over Sugar Loaf, as Mynydd Pen-y-fâl is more popularly known. With Skirrid (Ysgyryd Fawr) it is one of the most popular walking hills in the area, not surprisingly in view of its shape and the panorama from its peak. A sad by-product of this is the erosion of the pathways to the summit.

To reach Sugar Loaf take Pen-y-pound road out of the town centre, and then turn left into Avenue Road, which is followed slightly west of north to 289166. Here, bear left through Porth-y-parc Farm and on to a track that leads to open hillside, where the wayfarer enters National Trust land as much of Sugar Loaf is in possession of the Trust. To descend from the summit, go north-east to reach a track which leads to a minor road at (288204). Go left here, and bear right after 300 metres, to Five Ways (285211).

From here the route continues to Partrishow (Patrisio). The journey starts with the crossing of Pont yr Esgob (284211). Unfortunately the Ordnance Survey have changed the name to Pontysbig: the Welsh 'yr-Esgob' is correct, for this is the Bishop's Bridge. It is named for Archbishop Baldwin who was the travelling companion of Giraldus – or, more correctly, the reverse is true. Giraldus himself makes no mention of the bridge, or of nearby Partrishow. He notes that from Llan-ddew 'we made our way along the rugged pass of Coed Grwyne . . . by a narrow trackway overgrown with trees'. Giraldus may have been apprehensive of the journey as he notes that it was

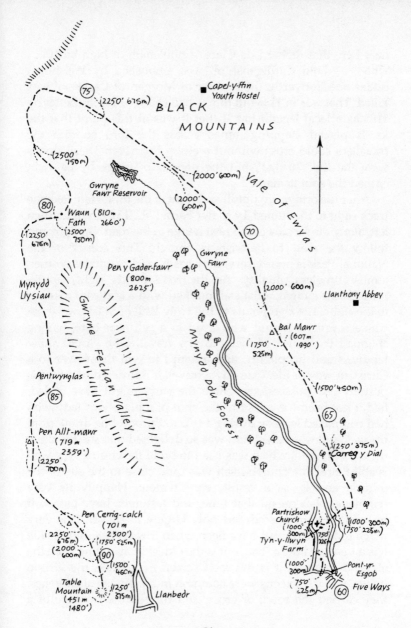

Capel-y-ffin
Youth Hostel

BLACK

MOUNTAINS

(75) (2250' 675m)

(2500' 750m)

Gwryne Fawr Reservoir

(2000' 600m) Vale of Ewyas

(2000' 600m)

(80) Waun Fach (810m 2660')

(2250' 676m)

(2500' 750m)

Mynydd Llysiau

Gwryne Fechan Valley

Pen y Gader-fawr (800m 2625')

Gwryne Fawr

(70)

(2000' 600m)

Llanthony Abbey

Bal Mawr (607m 1990')

(1750' 525m)

Pentwynglas (85)

Mynydd Ddu Forest

(1500' 450m)

Pen Allt-mawr (719m 2359')

(2250' 700m)

(65)

(1250' 375m)

Carreg y Dial

Pen Cerrig-calch (701m 2300')

(2250' 676m)

(1750' 525m)

(2000' 600m)

(90)

(1500' 460m)

Table Mountain (451m 1480')

(1250' 375m)

Llanbedr

Partrishow Church (1000' 300m)

(1000' 300m)

(750' 225m)

750' 225m

Ty'n-y-llwyn Farm

(1000' 300m)

Pont-yr-Esgob Five Ways

750' 225m

(60)

81

near here that Richard de Clare 'a nobleman of high birth . . . who . . . held Cardiganshire' was ambushed by Welshmen under one 'Iorwerth, the brother of Morgan of Caerleon' was killed. That was in 1136 but things had changed for the better by 1188 as a local legend has it that it was at this point that the locals placed stepping-stones across the ford so that the travellers could cross without wetting their feet. These stones were the first 'bridge', but the honour of usage by Baldwin earned the spot its name.

After the bridge, go uphill and right at the fork. Here take the track right to the ruined Tŷ Mawr Farm (282215). Go right, then left, along the far side of the next hedge to the road. Go right and follow the road to Partrishow church. This corner of the National Park is poorly served by roads, and maintains a quiet, almost timeless, quality. As the road bends right, uphill, towards the church, a flat slab marked with a Maltese cross lies to the right. The slab points to the Holy Well of St Ishow. Ishow was a mystic, a hermit who lived in a cell near here, having shunned the world of men. To any traveller he would show kindness and hospitality, and attempt to win them over to a Christian way of life. One day a traveller murdered him for his pitifully few possessions. There the story might have ended, had it not been for a visit to the spot of a high-born lady who had contracted leprosy during a trip to Europe. She drank from the well and was cured, and was so delighted that she filled the niches with gold, which was used to build the church. The well is still there. The church itself was built close to the site of the miracle and is, as a result, very remote. Happily its very remoteness has meant that time, and restorers, have passed it by, and, though altered and now largely medieval, it is very much today as it must have been when it was first built. Inside it is a treasure house. The font is the oldest item, dating from the eleventh century. It is the rood screen that draws the visitor, however. Such screens were common in the medieval churches; they carried the rood, or cross, and formed the frontage of a gallery that held the choir and, in earliest times, musicians. The gallery also allowed access to the rood itself so that it could be decorated with flowers during the various festivals throughout the year. This practice, as with murals and other 'idolatrous' ideas, appalled the Puritans and that, together with later, chiefly Victorian, vicars who wanted more space, caused the majority of screens and galleries to be removed. The almost complete screen here is therefore a major survival. It is also a masterpiece. The design is a repetition of a basic dragon and vine theme, probably to represent evil, the dragon, consuming good, the vine, but never finally triumphing because of the all-powerful good, represented by the cross that would have been fixed above. The work is said, with little or no supporting evidence, to be the work of an Italian woodcarver who was employed at nearby Llanthony Abbey.

It is hard to believe, when considering this work of art, that one of the reasons why the screen was extended to the floor – apart from the support this offered – and why altar rails were included in church designs after the discontinuation of screening, was to prevent dogs, who invariably accompanied their owners in the church, from fouling the altar!

A further medieval feature that would have incensed the Puritans is the fine mural on the west wall. This is a 'doom' figure, Father Time as a skeleton to represent death. Here it was painted near the exit so that the worshippers could see it as they departed, and so recognise their eventual fate and their only true salvation.

The church also retains a stone altar, in fact not one but two, each a memorial of the pre-Elizabethan days when the altar table was made from the tombstone of a martyr. At the time of Elizabeth it was ordered that such altars were to be destroyed and replaced by wooden tables, so the two here, at the base of the rood screen, are a remarkable find. Each has its five consecration crosses – one for each of the wounds of Christ. More remarkable still is the fact that the church actually has a third stone altar. This is situated in the odd little cell attached to the west wall. The room has a window allowing a view of the service, and may have been used by a particularly devout worshipper. Oddly, the altar in the cell has six crosses instead of the usual five.

The visitor will also notice the excellent cradle-roof of oak, and the stone benches that line the walls of the church. The latter were used by the old and sick in the days when there were no seats or pews in churches, and are the origin of the expression – 'the old go to the wall'. Altogether, Partrishow church is a most delightful place.

To continue, go eastward through the churchyard, and down the path to Ty'n-y-llwyn Farm (281223). From this track, looking back, the church is a fine sight, nestling in its shrub cover across the grass. Those who approach from this eastern side are offered a more spectacular first show, as only after they have visited the church are they likely to realise that it can be reached by road rather than by walking or riding across fields. After the farm building, a gate on the left gives access to an indistinct path, becoming less so, that leads directly to the road at (284226). Alternatively the farm lane can be followed down to the road at (284223). Go left to a road down to the river, and the chapel on its far side (284227). From the chapel, take a footpath north-east to a lane at (287229). The lane is followed to (289228) where the walker goes right on a track to Carreg y Dial (288228).

Carreg y Dial (the Stone of Revenge), was erected, so it is said, to commemorate the ambush and murder of Richard de Clare, an event mentioned earlier as having been recorded by Giraldus. De Clare had earlier made several attacks on the Welsh in order to secure further land, and was on his way to Cardigan. The local lord, Brian de Wallingford/Lille, accompanied de Clare as far as here to guide him through the 'pass', presumably the valley of the Grwyne Fawr. Despite de Wallingford's wishes and 'indeed, against his express advice' de Clare dismissed him and continued with only a small group of men. This would have been foolish enough, but de Clare sent ahead of the party a singer and fiddler to announce his coming. The party was ambushed and cut down, their baggage being stolen. After presenting the facts, Giraldus launches into an attack on those who are 'so presumptuous'. He reminds us that 'to rush on regardless is simply false bravado. It is at once rash and inconsiderate to take no heed at all of the advice given by those who are trying to help us.' This is not only a lesson from the Archdeacon, but Giraldus also talking as a good Norman for, shortly after de Clare's murder, the Welsh defeated the English at the Battle of Crug Mawr near Cardigan largely, or so says Giraldus, due to an absence of the leader (de Clare) on the English side. It is not clear who erected the stone, but it is certain that the present stone is not the first, an earlier one having been larger. Nor is it clear precisely where the ambush took place. Giraldus calls the wood simply Grwyne wood which would imply that it was in the valley at the foot of the ridge. Possibly the truth is that the association of stone and story is legendary, and that, as has been suggested, the stone is in fact an ancient sundial-cum-marker used by the Welsh cattle drovers en route for the Vale of Ewyas and Gospel Pass. The name would then have been 'deial' (for dial) instead of 'dial' (for revenge) though the two pronunciations are similar allowing considerable scope for the interchange. Beyond Carreg y Dial are the Black Mountains.

The Black Mountains

The Black Mountains are the most easterly of the blocks of Old Red Sandstone peaks that make up the Brecon Beacons National Park. As with the other blocks the most characteristic feature is the escarpment, here facing north-west, although there are no corrie lakes, and the area is split by striking valleys. The valleys run north/south, draining down to the Usk valley, and so deep have they cut into the sandstone mass that they have created a series of parallel ridges. To the east is the Hatterrall Hill to Hay

Bluff ridge, taken by the Offa's Dyke long-distance footpath, separated by the magnificent Vale of Ewyas from the main mass of the Mountains. In this main mass there is a continuous ridge-top to the escarpment, the valleys of Afonydd Grwyne Fawr and Grwyne Fechan having failed to cut back to the escarpment itself. The geography is, therefore, of a trident, with three prongs ending at Bâl Mawr, Crug Mawr and Pen Cerrig Calch. To the west there is a small outlying group of peaks lying between the stream and Llangorse Lake (Llyn Syfaddan). The ridges created by these valleys are wide and whale-backed, the valleys themselves being wooded and having a secluded, peaceful air.

Though the Mountains comprise wide grassy ridges, there are some peat deposits which, particularly at the summit of Waun Fach, create difficult walking where the peat is deeply trenched and wet. Despite this the ridges make walking relatively safe, but the traveller should beware, for in addition to all the dangers that may befall the unwary in bad weather, there is also the 'old lady' of the Black Mountains, a spectral figure who may appear to lead him astray.

As well as peat there are heather beds, particularly to the north, which attract large numbers of butterflies. Because of the heavily-grazed grassland that predominates, the upland birdlife is chiefly limited to members of the crow and lark families. In the valleys, the situation is much improved, the Grwyne Fawr stream holding a number of dippers and grey wagtails, while the mixed woodland at stream level attracts a great variety of small birds.

From Carreg y Dial the route continues straightforwardly to Garn-wen, and on to Bâl Mawr. From there, a reasonable path leads on along the ridge towards the escarpment. To the east from here, and well worth the walk to the ridge edge, is the Vale of Ewyas. This has long been the favourite among the valleys that bury themselves deep into the Black Mountains, one reason being that at its head there is a pass between the peaks of

Twmpa and Hay Bluff. This is Gospel Pass, named from a straightforward translation of Bwlch yr Efengyl. The Welsh name derives from a legend that a daughter of Caratacus (Caradog), the Silurian leader at the time of the Roman invasion, invited St Peter and St Paul to come and preach the gospel to her people. They came, and in their journey to, or from, the Usk valley they used this pass.

Another reason that the Ewyas vale is famous is because of its beauty. The high ridge from Hatterrall Hill to Hay Bluff to the east, and the present ridge to the west, ensure for the valley a wonderful quiet and calm, as well as giving a wonderful backdrop to any view in the valley itself. The view to the east of Bâl Mawr is dominated by the ruins of Llanthony Priory. The ruins are impressive, and although they may not have the completeness or the dignity of nearby Tintern Abbey, they are wonderfully positioned. It is easy to see why William de Lacy, the founder, chose to stay when he came here towards the end of the twelfth century weary, or so it is said, of his life of vice and sin. De Lacy is said to have worn his armour as a hair shirt until it rusted and fell off with age. There was a church here even at that time, but de Lacy wanted a more profoundly spiritual environment – in keeping with the serenity of the site perhaps – and founded an Augustinian priory. Giraldus recounts a story about the building of the priory in the first person, suggesting that he may have been a party to it. The priory, he says, was built with blocks of 'marble' called freestones that were to be found lying on the mountain-side, and 'they have this remarkable property, that you can search until you are quite exhausted and collect all these freestones, until none is left and no more could possibly be found, and then, three or fours days later, you can look again and there they all are, just as numerous as before, easy to find if you look, and there for you to take'.

Those heading for the Youth Hostel at Capel-y-ffin can ascend the Vale of Ewyas without regaining the ridge. The 'main' road need not be taken, as a minor road also ascends the valley on the eastern side of the river. For those who have not visited Llanthony, beyond Bâl Mawr the route is easy, towards the escarpment. It is best at the northern end to avoid the temptation to contour around the head of cwm Grwyne Fawr the apparent distance that can be saved being more than made up for in the time lost on unremitting vegetation. The tracks, badly eroded by pony-trekkers who appear from time to time in 7th Cavalry numbers, do at least offer reasonable walking. The wayfarer is now heading for Waun Fach (the 'little moor') that is the highest point of the range. It is not the 'high point', the summit lying in the middle of a small peat bog, though this is of little consequence as the ground for many metres in all directions is at the same altitude. South-east from Waun Fach is the only real peak on the range, Pen y Gadair Fawr, a fine summit with a good cairn. Those who wish to include the peak can continue along the path beside the forestry plantations to Crug Mawr, from where a track leads down to the village of Llanbedr. From there a minor road leads down to Crickhowell (Crucywel). The better route is to follow the ridge that leads south from Pen Trumau, a top to the west of Waun Fach. The ridge is followed to Pen-allt Mawr, a steep climb preceding the summit. This is, perhaps, the best ridge walk in South Wales, and rivals many an expedition in the north. The walking is never strenuous, though sometimes a little difficult, and the views are superb.

Because the ridge is a very wide whale-back, the eye is drawn away from the immediate valleys, which are a little hidden below the curve of the land, to the distant hills, plains and valleys. The Black Mountains horseshoe walk – starting from Llanbedr and going out via Crug Mawr and Pen y Gadair Fawr to Waun Fach, and returning along this ridge – is understandably popular, and deserves inclusion in any Welsh walker's itinerary.

The route from Pen-allt Mawr continues along the ridge to Pen Cerrig Calch, an interesting peak as its summit is the final surviving section of the limestone sheet that once overlaid the sandstone to the north of the Usk, and still does on the Llangattock (Llangatwg) escarpment south of the river. The name is descriptive of this limestone cap, evidence of the understanding the early Welsh farmers had of their land, before the science of geology revealed the existence and significance of this outlying sheet. From the limestone cap, the wayfarer makes his way down east of south to the obvious feature of Table Mountain which, as will be mentioned later, is defined by the remains of the hill-fort after which the town of Crickhowell is named. From the southern edge of the flat-topped peak descend south-west to a house (Dôl-y-Gaer) from where a track, waymarked beyond the house, leads south to a farm (Wern), and on to a minor road which is followed into Crickhowell.

Crickhowell (Crucywel)

Crickhowell lies in the shadow of Table Mountain, not as famous as its South African counterpart perhaps but just as well named. The proper spelling is Crucywel, Hywel's hill, said to derive from Hywel Dda (Hywel the Good) the famous law-giver whose statue is amongst those of the Welsh heroes in Cardiff's Civic Centre. Hywel was an early tenth-century leader, and it is possible that the hill-fort that stands on top of the hill was still occupied around that time. Its general layout is typically Iron Age, which would mean that it pre-dated Hywel by a thousand years. The length and steepness of the approach on all but the northern side must have made the fort a formidable site, and its position in the lower part of the Usk valley, guarding the valley itself, was also crucial. The Normans with their improved castle building techniques could afford to place a lord at Tretower (Tretŵr), the more strategically correct site, but they did not ignore Crucywel. The ruins we now see in the town are those of the castle built by a later lord, with the unlikely name of Sir Grimbaud Pauncefoot, in the latter part of the thirteenth century. It was Sir Grimbaud's wife, Lady Sybil, who was co-founder of Crickhowell's church and it is believed that the effigies within it, at the side of the altar, are of the Knight and his Lady. It is interesting that with England under Norman rule, the dedication of the church was to St Edmund, the adopted son of Offa the Saxon King, who built the dyke between England and Wales. In its complete form Crickhowell's castle had a shell keep, as at Tretower, around a motte from an original construction, and a wall with towers from later phases of work. Additions were being made right up to the time of the Glyndŵr revolt, but following that, when the castle was almost completely destroyed, there was neither renovation nor addition. Thereafter the site became a dependable and easily accessible quarry, and as lately as the 1900s there was a major collapse. Now all that remain are the ivy-clad ruins of the gatehouse tower and portcullis gate. The old motte is known affectionately as The Tump, while the whole has acquired the name Alisby's Castle, from a later owner.

Using the castle as a starting point, the traveller will be well rewarded for the effort of taking a short walk around the town. In Castle Street is the Presbyterian Danycastell chapel. Now go across the top of Bridge Street and through Lamb Lane to New Road. To the left here is a building that was once a flannel mill, Crickhowell having once been an important manufacturing centre, as was nearby Abergavenny. To the right is the church of St Edmund. Little of the building dates from the first mentioned period, and there was considerable restoration in the nineteenth century. Much that is fine remains, however, particularly the reredos and some of the earlier windows. Neither has the restoration been without its successes. This is especially true of the spire that was rebuilt in 1861 to the design of J Pearson, the architect of some of the restorations of Westminster Abbey. Unhappily the financing of the spire was not as harmonious as the design and caused considerable local argument and, eventually, reached the courts. Continuing up New Road the traveller arrives at the main A40. To the left here is Porth Mawr, the Big Gate. Indeed it is a large castellated gatehouse, finely set in a length of solid stone wall. Behind this imposing structure there is – nothing! At one time there was of course, but Cwrt-y-Carw (Stag Court), built in Tudor times for the Hubert family, has long since gone. West from here is Gwernvale, once a manor house, now a hotel, in which was born in 1790, Sir George Everest whose name is now world famous having been given to a mountain when it was discovered to be the highest in the world, while Sir George was Surveyor-General of India. Turning right at Porth Mawr the traveller heads back towards the centre of the town passing the Bear Hotel, another of the coaching inns that lined the Usk valley route down to the Severn. It is thought that the imposing Georgian front is superimposed on an older building. Our route now goes through the Square and down High Street to the steep Bridge Street. This is from the eighteenth century, and is complete with cobbled pavements and bow-fronted shops. At the bottom is the Bridge End Inn whose wrap-around look derives from the foundations of the Octagonal Toll House, on which it stands. The bridge itself is one of the high points of a trip around the town. The present one dates, in the main, from 1706 when it was stone-built at a cost of £400. When it was first widened and then modified to accept the New Road in the early nineteenth century, the bridge acquired an imbalance. If the traveller checks, he will discover that there are 13 arches on one side, but only 12 on the other.

Llangattock and Chartists' Cave

Beyond the bridge is Llangattock (Llangatwg), a little south of which the Brecon and Abergavenny Canal is reached again. Here, as at Llanfoist (Llan-ffwyst), there are lime-kilns. Initially, as a study of the Llangattock escarpment by wayfarers who visit it will show, the kilns were at the quarries. With the advent of improved transport however, it was decided to move stone to the canal by tramway, to create the kilns at the wharves, and then ship out the prepared lime. The kilns at Llangattock were by a tramway that came down inclines from the escarpment quarries. Lime was also carried to the ironworks at Beaufort. The village itself is a quiet place, ambling gently back up the hill towards the escarpment that takes its name. The name derives from St Catwg, another of the many early Celtic Christians, and the church to him is interesting in still possessing, inside, the old village stocks and whipping-post.

From Llangattock, the suggested route follows the minor road south, or the track that exits south from it at the left-hand bend (206169), to the Llangattock escarpment. On Mynydd Llangatwg and Mynydd Llangynidr the rights of way run north/south, not east/west, but there is considerable literature on east/west crossings, and many walkers tramp the moorland at weekends. The right-of-way route from here follows the canal tow-path to Llangynidr, as detailed above.

The escarpment itself is interesting, far beyond the industrial archaeology of the kilns and tramway. Here the limestone 'bursts out along the whole range of mountains' as it was said in 1805, and that is true for the escarpment reveals the limestone from under the millstone cover. Above the cliffs there are a large number of instances where the caves in the underlying limestone have collapsed, causing sink or swallow holes. In addition, the impervious millstone has allowed some hollows to fill with water, causing ponds to appear where the wayfarer does not expect ponds to be. One such is Pwll Gwrach, the witches' pond. That is just how it feels, for on this stretch of moorland the visitor is usually alone, and it is surprising to come upon this large, dark stretch of water, its edges half-hidden among the bilberries. In the right conditions of wind and mist, it would come as no surprise to hear the cackling laughter of Macbeth's witches.

The western end of the escarpment forms the Craig y Cilau Nature Reserve, set up to protect its plant life. Here there are many fine limestone plants that are found in few other places in Britain. The chief interest, however, lies in the six very rare

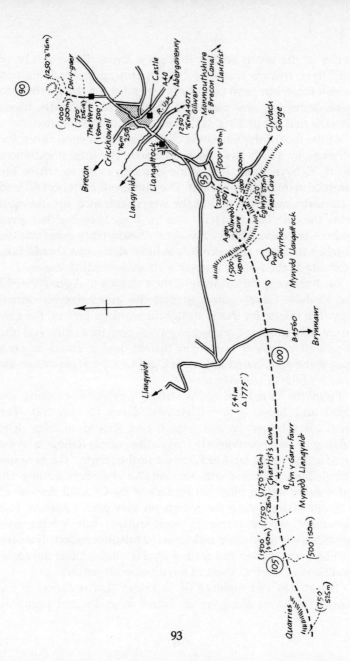

species of the genus sorbus that grow there. These shrubs or small trees, rowans and whitebeams, grow, in general, high on the cliff faces, but great care should be taken by the wayfarer to avoid damaging any plant life in the area. It hardly needs stressing that the picking of flowers is out of the question.

At the foot of the limestone cliffs there are several caves, the entrances to which have been quarried. The largest entrances are of 'Eglwys Faen' (the stone church), close to where the tramroad swings sharply right. The numerous entrances all lead to the same cave system, but the largest entrance, up and right facing the cliff, leads directly into the huge chamber that gives the cave its name. The wayfarer can comfortably penetrate the chamber for some distance in daylight alone, but should take great care as the floor is littered with ankle-turning stones.

Farther along the pathway is the entrance to Agen Allwedd (the Keyhole Cave), gated so that the inexperienced cannot enter. The reason for this is straightforward for beyond the gate are 29 kilometres of passageway. At one time this was the longest cave system known in Britain, and it could be once again if the anticipated link with Ogof Craig y Ffynnon, on the far side of the hill, is ever made.

From the caves the route strikes westward, crossing the B4560 and heading for Chartists' Cave at (127152). The moorland is barren here and great care should be taken. The walking is not particularly easy, the whole being a good introduction to the land of Elenydd farther north. The cave has a single large chamber with two smaller chambers leading off, and was the hiding place for leaders of the Chartist movement in South Wales before the march on Newport. Chartism is a movement whose name is well-known, but whose true significance is most often unknown or misunderstood. The cave is still a good shelter and resting spot to contemplate the social conditions of the first third of the nineteenth century.

The strikes and upsurge of unionism that occurred in the mining and ironmaking communities were directed primarily against the poverty of men's working lives, but contained an element of resentment against the existing social order. The Poor Law of 1834 with its workhouses and, more importantly, the idea that the poor were responsible for, and should be made to suffer for, their poverty caused unrest. Few of those in power had any sympathy with Cobbett's idea that a pauper was only a very poor man, and the unsympathetic nature of their law caused great resentment in those affected. After the years of bad working and living conditions, repression by force if necessary, and injustice, resentment boiled over and became a movement that touched every part of Britain. The movement was known as Chartism because its followers supported the People's Charter published in 1838, a six-point plan for Parliamentary reform which demanded universal male suffrage; equal electoral districts; secret ballots; abolition of property qualifications for Members of Parliament; payment of Members; and annual Parliaments. Now, with five points of the Charter accepted and the sixth, annual parliaments, not felt to be a practical proposition by any credible organisation, it is difficult to understand the threat to the established order that the demands represented.

In South Wales the Chartist' leader was John Frost, a man of fifty-five in the fateful year of 1839. By 1839 the Chartists' leaders became convinced that attempts to achieve some reforms, or even discussion of their grievances, were doomed to failure and some began to argue in favour of direct action. A general strike was called for August, but this never occurred. Eventually in November Frost, convinced that the men of the Midlands and North of England were ready to rise up and seize power, decided to give the lead by organising the men of South Wales to capture Newport. In secret he advised local leaders and soon there were men hiding in wait in this cave, and others in the caves of the Llangatwg escarpment, making weapons. On 3 November all was ready and the men started to make their way into the Ebbw valley and down it to Risca. The weather was appalling and far fewer men than expected arrived at the town. They were also badly armed, many having only pitchforks with them. Frost had hoped to be able to command as many as 50,000 men but he had many fewer than that. The Chartists themselves later claimed it was as few as 400, though the Mayor of Newport claimed 20,000. Neither figure is likely to be correct with each side exaggerating to its own ends, and it is likely that Frost had 5,000 men when he arrived at Newport on 4 November. The Mayor assumed command of the small band of soldiers, about thirty in number, in the town and stationed them at the Westgate Hotel. There was an exchange of words between the two sides, but communication in the real sense was beyond hope. A shot was fired, each side claiming, after, that the other fired first, and the soldiers immediately fired a volley into the crowd, continuing to fire haphazardly for about ten minutes more. The Chartists, not surprisingly in view of their condition, turned and fled, leaving twenty-two men behind, dead or dying. Frost was captured soon after and was tried with seven other local leaders for treason. They were found guilty and sentenced to death by hanging, that to be followed by decapitation and quartering. In order to avoid a sympathetic backlash the sentences were commuted, and Frost was transported to Van Diemen's Land. Fifteen years later Frost was pardoned and returned to Britain white-haired, but still a strong-willed man. He died in 1877 at the great age of 93.

Following the Newport rebellion Chartism declined in Wales, not surprisingly as a great number of people were appalled by the uprising, regardless of its justification. From 1839 onwards, the workers followed the less dangerous pathway of local strikes.

Our route continues across trackless and difficult ground towards the Beacons. There is little shelter here and few landmarks, even the cave being easy to miss if conditions are less than perfect. Head west, but go south of the quarries of Pistyll Crawnon. A right of way goes north of these on the southern edge of the forest, but this involves crossing fences where the right of way ends. The southern route keeps to open moorland traversing above the quarries to (085148). From here go north-west, heading for a landmark, the summit of Pant y Creigiau at 056162. This latter section is marshy, but offers an expanding view of the Brecon Beacons. From the summit, descent is made to the minor road at (050167) where the route from the canal tow-path is rejoined. Continue easily to the Neuadd Reservoirs and the Brecon Beacons.

The Brecon Beacons

The mass of the Brecon Beacons is the most distinctive in the National Park, the truncated summits of Corn Du and Pen y Fan being easily distinguished from almost any direction. The scenery here is similar to Waun Fach, on the Black Mountains in the eastern section of the mass, where it forms a plateau at around 730m (2,400ft) which extends over about 2.5 sq kms (1 sq mile) around Gwaun Cerrig Llwydion and Waen Rydd. Here the peat outcrops are so deep that the walker can trek between them in an almost lunar landscape. This is an isolated example of true similarity, however, for the Beacons are characterised more by the glacially-hollowed U-valleys to the north than by river valleys. Particularly fine is Cwm Oergwm, to the east of Pen y Fan itself. The escarpment face, particularly on the higher peaks, also appears more precipitous and this, together with the corrie lake, Llyn Cwm-llwch, gives the mass a more mountainous, less pastoral quality.

The route follows the Roman road towards the pass to the east of Cribyn, before moving off left (west) to follow the (too) well-marked path up to Pen y Fan summit. This is the highest peak in South Wales, and fails by only 93 feet to be the fifteenth 3,000-foot peak in Wales. There is no denying the very real attraction of Pen y Fan, the steep northern face more than making up, from a 'mountain' point of view, for the curious flat top, but the popularity of it can detract from its attractiveness if it is swarming with weekend walkers. This is a sad, but necessary, by-product of freedom of access.

From the summit of Pen y Fan and nearby Corn Du the view is extensive, over mid-Wales to Pumlumon and over South Wales. From Corn Du there are several ways off to the west. Those going to the Youth Hostel can go north-west down the ridge that passes the Tommy Jones memorial obelisk at 000217. Tommy was the five-year-old son of a Welsh miner who came to the Beacons in 1900 to visit his grandfather. They were walking from Brecon when they met the boy's grandfather and cousin. Tommy and his cousin ran ahead to the grandfather's farm, but after a short distance the boy ran back to rejoin his father. He never arrived and an extensive search failed to locate him. It was almost a month later that his body was found at this spot, a long way from where he was last seen. At the time the disappearance was headline news but doubtless it would now be forgotten if the obelisk had not been erected. It is a timely reminder of the risk inherent in a walk over the Welsh mountains by anyone, of any age.

Those not going down to the Youth Hostel can descend south-west to reach the A470 to the south of the Storey Arms. Immediately to the west of the A470 now is Fforest Fawr, the Great Forest of the Lords of Brecon. As usual, the word forest here causes confusion at a time when forest for most of us means regimented rows of conifers. In medieval times a forest was simply a hunting ground. Now the name is applied to the moorland between the A470 and A4067, containing the distinctive peaks of Fan Fawr to the east and Fan Gyhirych to the west. On Ordnance Survey maps, the name is applied also to the land in Y Mynydd Du, as far as Fan Hir, which conforms to the official Norman forest. From the A470 near the Storey Arms the ascent of Fan Fawr is straightforward, and is accomplished by numbers of walkers each weekend. It is equally straightforward to continue westward around the northern end of the Ystradfellte reservoir over Fan Llia to the

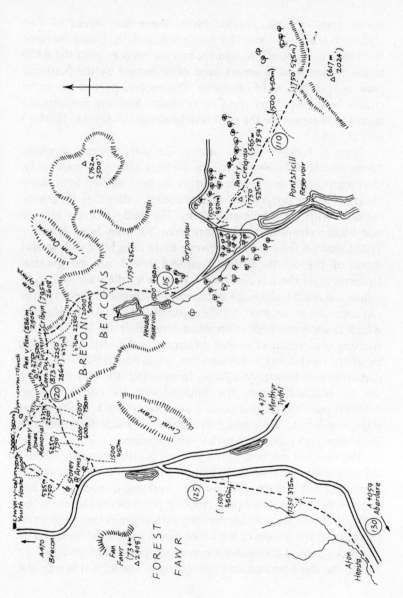

99

minor road around 924194. From there the ascent of Fan Gyhirych is accomplished by going north of Fan Nedd. None of this route is on public footpaths, but the section from the A470 to the minor road is across land now owned by the National park, and so has right of access. The second part of the route covers land owned by the Cnewr estate. Walkers are allowed access here except for the period of lambing (15 April to 10 May) and at night.

There is, however, a fine alternative to this mountain route. To the south of Fforest Fawr the scenery changes remarkably, the escarpments and grassed ridges of the Old Red Sandstone giving way to deeply cut and wooded valleys of limestone country, with waterfalls and caves. The valleys of the Hepste and Mellte rivers are little more than 10 miles from Merthyr Tydfil, and yet the contrast between these delightful valleys and those of the South Wales Coalfield could not be greater. Unfortunately there is no other way to enter the valleys than to follow the A4059, although as the road is unfenced the wayfarer can cross the moorland on either side of the road. Afon Hepste, which is soon reached, is an interesting river, for long periods running underground so that its stream bed is dry. A short cut, by minor road direct to Ystradfellte, is reached at 944105 a short distance from Penderyn village, from which the Hepste valley can be reached. Leave the village from its northern edge (944089) past houses and on to a signposted track, going to the right, not left, to Tir-y-foel Farm. Take the track downhill into the valley, and follow the valley downstream.

The first fall reached, Sgwd yr Eira, is also the most famous, because the visitor can walk behind the curtain of water which is pushed out 1 metre (3ft) by the overhang of rock at the fall head. This is, in fact, the only crossing point of the Hepste in the valley and was used at one time by farmers moving sheep from one side of the valley to the other. Great care must be taken as the rocks behind the water are very slippery. Though Sgwd yr Eira is the most famous and interesting of the falls, it is only the

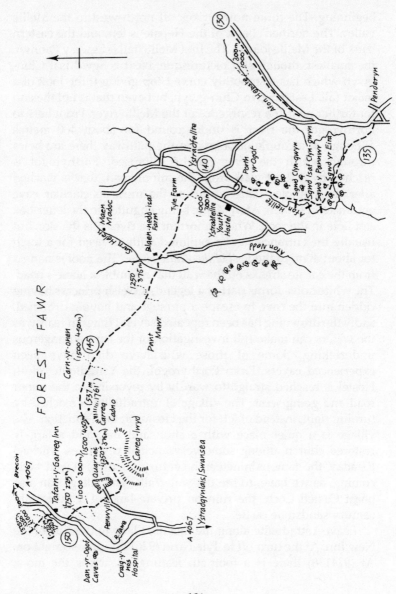

beginning. The route now strikes off north-west to the Mellte valley. The northern bank of the Hepste is left, and the eastern bank of the Mellte joined. The first Mellte fall is Sgwd y Pannwr, the smallest, though still picturesque. Next is Sgwd Isaf Clungwyn which has a smoothly curved top giving it the look of a major fall. Last is Sgwd Clun-gwyn, but even that is not the end for farther on is the resurgence of the Mellte river. From here to Porthyrogof the river is underground for about 400 metres although at a couple of points on the pathway there are holes through which the river can be glimpsed. Porthyrogof is reached by a short walk from the minor road, that is reached after the potholes. This is one of the most spectacular cave entrances in Britain, Afon Mellte being engulfed in the letter-box slot hole in the rock. When in torrent the river fills the slot, but usually the entrance can be explored without need for a torch for about 40m, to the *Pool of the White Horse*. The pool is named from the calcite streaks on the wall that resemble a horse's head. The white horse forms part of a legend, a Welsh princess having ridden into the cave to escape a pursuer and having drowned. Sadly the drowning has been repeated several times in reality, as the waters can make full investigation of the cave a dangerous undertaking. Some of those who have died have been experienced cavers. From Porthyrogof, the Ystradfellte Youth Hostel is reached straightforwardly by reversing to the minor road and going west. The village of Ystradfellte is reached by turning right, instead of left for the Hostel, at the T-junction. The village is a quiet place with a shop and inn, and a largely restored church among some very ancient yew trees. Michael Faraday, the famous nineteenth-century scientist, stayed here, coming, as we have, to see the waterfalls. The village can also boast Castell Coch, the ruin on private land of a thirteenth-century sandstone castle.

Leave Ystradfellte along the metalled lane to the side of the New Inn. At the turn-off to Tyle Farm (926134) carry straight on. At (924138) there is a footpath leading off across the moor, and go north of west to a minor road at (913142). Turn right towards Blaen-nedd-isaf Farm. A footpath is signposted westward over a footbridge to the south of the farm. This footpath soon crosses Sarn Helen, a Roman road reputedly named after a Welsh princess – whom we shall encounter again at Croesor in Snowdonia, as we near the end of our journey.

Beyond the Roman road there is excellent walking on open moor to the quarries at Pen-wyllt (856156). Under the quarries is Ogof Ffynnon Ddu, the cave of the black spring. There are three entrances to the cave, widely separated, the separation giving some idea of what lies below the surface. For here is a cave system which, at 38km, is one of the longest in Britain and, at 300m, also one of the deepest. Not only is it enormous, but it is also extremely complex having what is widely believed to be the most dazzling three-dimensional array of passages of any cave in Britain. Not surprisingly it is kept locked, the key being given only to established caving clubs.

The wayfarer may follow the old, now trackless, railway line to the head of the minor road at Pen-wyllt (854158), or he may go directly for the road, which is unfenced on its south-eastern side around the quarry at 851155. Now either take a south-westerly route down towards Afon Tawe, and then swing northwards to reach and cross the river and hence reach the A4067 at 842160, or go almost due north to Pwll-coediog (849164) and follow the lane to the A4067. The decision depends upon whether he wishes to visit Dan yr Ogof show caves and Dinosaur Park.

A little down the valley from Dan yr Ogof is Craig-y-nos Castle started in 1842, but completed by the famous opera singer Dame Adelina Patti during her residence from 1879 until her death in 1919.

Leaving the caves the wayfarer goes north along the A4067 to reach the second route at 847167. Continue north again to the Tafarn y Garreg Inn. Opposite it, a footpath is signed to a new bridge over Afon Tawe, and Mynydd Du beyond.

Y Mynydd Du

The name Mynydd Du is the Welsh original name for Black Mountain, the lack of the plural 's' being the only way of distinguishing this most westerly sandstone mass from the eastern Black Mountains. This is the most mysterious and desolate of the Beacons' masses. Its northern edge has the, by now, usual escarpment and here it is both very steep and very long, and continues along the eastern edge of the mass, so that it broods over the lakes Llyn y Fan Fawr and Llyn y Fan Fach. Behind the scarp, however, lies a shallow dip slope that extends a considerable distance westward and southward to form an upland plateau, in places boggy, that has a wild and desolate air. This almost featureless plateau is land for the connoisseur. To add to the mystery there are a number of *menhirs* in the area and, in addition, at Cerrig Duon (851206), one of the few Welsh stone alignments. The site consists of a circle of small stones, some 60cms (2ft) high, about 18m (60ft) in diameter with an avenue of stones leading away to the north-east and a single large stone, 2m (6ft) high, 10m to the north. The stones have been vandalised by name-scratchers, but the site has a distinct atmosphere, assisted doubtless, by its wind-swept nature and the backdrop of the long ridge of Fan Hir.

Cerrig Duon is worth visiting, though this sadly means a detour. After the site, however, things improve significantly, the wayfarer following Nant y Llyn back to Llyn y Fan Fawr, ascending the slope to Bannau Brycheiniog, and continuing around the escarpment until above Llyn y Fan Fach. Here, though steep, the scarp slope is easily descended to the lakeside.

The last route description does indeed offer the best continuation, those not visiting Cerrig Duon continuing from the Tawe bridge up Fan Hir to the summit. This is a much travelled and published route though the only true right of way crosses the southern moorland heading north-west and then north to Llanddeusant. This route should be treated with great caution. The area crossed is difficult and desolate, and it is also

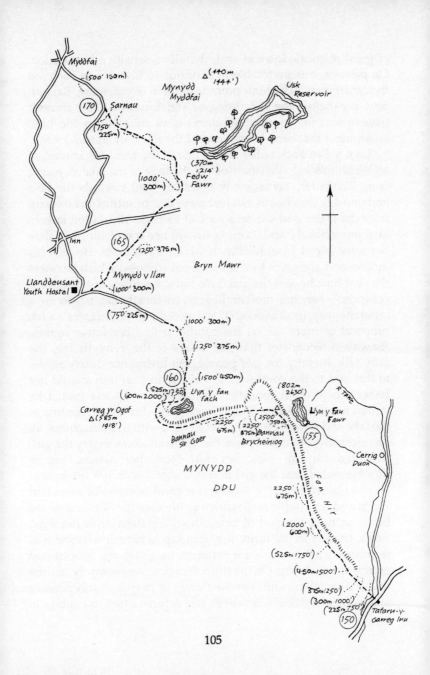

Myddfai

(500' 150m)

Sarnau

(750' 225m)

170

Mynydd
Myddfai

△ (440 m
1444')

Usk
Reservoir

(370m
1214')
Fedw
Fawr

(1000'
300m)

Inn

165

(1250' 375m)

Bryn Mawr

Mynydd y llan

(1000' 300m)

Llanddeusant
Youth Hostel ■

(750' 225m)

(1000' 300m)

(1250' 375m)

(1500' 450m)

160

(525m1750)

(600m 2000)

Llyn y fan
fach

(802m
2630')

(2250
675m)

(2500)

Carreg yr Ogof
△ (585m
1918')

Bannau
Sir Gaer

(2250
875m)
Bannau
Brycheiniog

(2250
750m)

R. TAWE

Llyn y Fan
Fawr

155

Cerrig O
Duon

MYNYDD

DDU

2250'
675m

Fan Hir

(2000'
600m)

(525m 1750)

(450m 1500)

(375m 1250)

(300m 1000)

(225m 750)

150

Tafarn-y-
Garreg Inn

of great scientific interest and, therefore, sensitive to invasion. On balance, it is preferable to continue to Llyn y Fan Fach via the escarpment. The high point is Bannau Brycheiniog. Bannau Sir Gaer (before the redefining of Welsh counties, the summit plateau was the county boundary) is an arc of steep and high escarpment that broods over one of the finest of lakeland sites.

Llyn y Fan Fach is the site of one of the most fascinating of all Welsh folk legends, the story of the lady of the lake. A young man, Rhiwallon, occasionally takes his herd towards the lake and one day watches in astonishment as a beautiful girl rises up from the water and sits on a rock at its edge. Rhiwallon falls in love immediately and, hoping to win her friendship, he offers her some bread from his lunch which she refuses. He tells his mother and she gives him some unbaked bread which he offers the next time he sees the girl. This too she refuses, but on a third occasion when his mother has given him bread baked in a different way (unleavened?), she accepts it and agrees to his proposal of marriage on the condition that her father agrees. Rhiwallon recognises that she is one of the Tylwyth Teg, the fairy folk, literally the fair people, but loving her dearly agrees to this and to the condition that she places on him should her father accept. That condition is that she will leave him if he strikes her three times. The following day Rhiwallon returns to the lake and from it emerges an old man with five daughters, all identical. The old man agrees that Rhiwallon can marry the girl, provided he can pick her out from her sisters. He is dumbfounded, but the girl makes a signal with her toe so that he can choose her. Her dowry is a great number of oxen and sheep and the couple settle down to life together. Three sons are born but, over a period of time, Rhiwallon does strike her three times, usually in the form of a light tap to correct what he sees as incorrect behaviour – for instance, laughing at a funeral and crying at a wedding. On the third occasion she promptly returns to the lake, taking with her the dowry of oxen and sheep. Since she is a good mother, however, she returns often to explain to her growing sons the secret of fairy medicines, and they grow up to be fine healers and form the basis of a line of doctors stretching through history.

The story is not so greatly different from other folk tales, and even from some of the stories in the Mabinogion, but there are subtle parts to it that suggest it is based on not only truth, but on a quite remarkable folk memory. When the iron-using Celts first moved into Wales, in the final millennium BC, they would have encountered a people who were largely of New Stone Age culture, even if they possessed bronze implements. Some of these people were Mediterranean in origin and would have been short and dark-skinned, as indeed some Welsh people are today. There are several different versions of the story, though all agree on the salient details, but in the longer and more local versions the girl's relatives are short and dark, and they visit Rhiwallon's people's market on occasions, though they converse in sign language as they cannot speak his people's language. It is known that the older culture did, on occasions, live in the lake communities, on semi-floating platforms which made it appear, perhaps, that the people could rise out of the water. Rhiwallon has problems selecting the girl – because all foreigners look the same! – and in some versions he must not strike her with iron, a taboo that could be expected in non-iron-using cultures. Her excellence in teaching her sons to be healers could come from the older culture's cleverness in the use of herbal remedies.

Seen in this light what was an old folk tale, pleasant but shallow, becomes a remarkable tale of the touching of two cultures many, many centuries ago. It would indeed be good if the story did represent the coming of the Celts to Wales, as the implication of the story is that the culture shock was minimal and that the Celts mingled with the original settlers, rather than destroying them out of hand as has so often happened in the history of advanced societies meeting relatively backward ones.

The escarpment cliffs can give the lake an air of mystery on cold, misty days, but in summer it is a delightful place alive with the calls of meadow pipits parachuting to earth, and with the flashes of sandpipers beating across the moorland. The lake water is a breeding ground for a large number of eels, the people who consume the two million gallons that it supplies each day being presumably unaware that both eels and fairies inhabit their water supply.

From the lake, follow the water company road north towards Llanddeusant, a hamlet whose church has some fourteenth-century features. Before Llanddeusant, at 779246, a track right can be followed to common land on Mynydd y Llan. Go north-east, crossing the road, to the flank of Fedw Fawr (802274). Turning north-west we head across the moor to a path at 785285 which is followed to Sarnau (783290). Follow the road into Myddfai. Those who, at Llanddeusant, are interested in a change of scenery can follow the road all the way to Myddfai. At first sight this does not seem a good option, but it is as the lanes are a delight.

Myddfai

Myddfai is the reputed home of Rhiwallon, the finest of the physician sons of the lady of the lake. Rhiwallon was named after his father and started the line of physicians in the town. This line is known to have lasted at least six hundred years, and regardless of whether its actual starting was supernatural or not, that is a remarkable achievement for so small a village. The first doctor known to have lived in the area was the twelfth-century physician to the local lord, and he was actually called Rhiwallon. For references to later members of the line it is necessary only to look at the memorials in the church, or at the local place-names. The church has many memorials to surgeons and physicians, the last being to one who died in 1842 in Aberystwyth. In the area there are farms named for the *meddygon* (physicians), Evan and Meredith, as well as a Physician's Gate where, reputedly, the lake lady handed her knowledge on to Rhiwallon. An interesting part of the story is

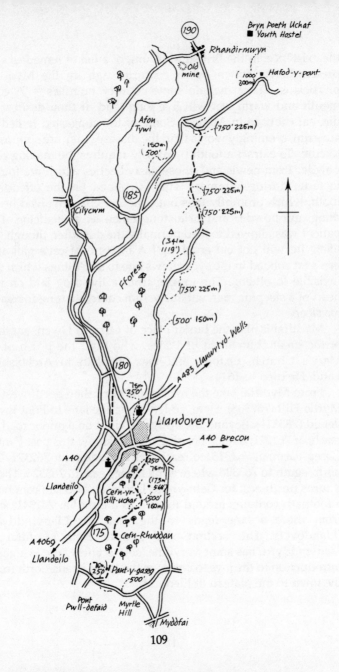

Bryn Poeth Uchaf
■ Youth Hostel

190

Rhandirmwyn

Old mine

(1000' 300m) ■ Hafod-y-pant

Afon Tywi

(150m 500')

(750' 225m)

185

(750' 225m)

Cilycwm

(750' 225m)

△ (341m 1119')

Fforest

(750' 225m)

(500' 150m)

180

A483 Llanwrtyd-Wells

(75m 250')

Llandovery

A40 Brecon

A40

(250' 76m)

Llandeilo

(173m 566')

Cefn-yr-allt-uchar

(500' 160m)

A4069

Cefn-Rhuddan

Llandeilo

(76m 250')

Pant-y-gaseg
(500')

Pont Pwll-defaid

Myrtle Hill

I Myddfai

the existence, in the British Museum, of a list of remedies and prescriptions written down centuries ago by the Myddfai physicians. These include some country homilies – 'A cold mouth and warm feet will live long' and 'If thou desirest to die, eat cabbage in August'. Some of the suggested remedies are grim, seemingly worse than the diseases they are supposed to cure. To extract a tooth painlessly requires the making of a powder from newts and 'those nasty beetles which are found in ferns during summer'. This is rubbed on the offending tooth, which promptly falls out. Another cure involved hen's dung, gunpowder and brimstone taken as a medicine. The patient was allowed to feed normally the day after, though 'tis likely he will not eat anything'! A mixture of cat's gall and hen's fat rubbed in the eyes allows one to see 'things which are invisible to others'. The tongue from a live frog laid on the heart of a sleeping man will make him confess wrongdoings in his sleep.

Myddfai is also the burial place of Morgan Owen, another of the great churchmen of Wales, who built the porch of St Mary's Church, Oxford, and was chaplain to Archbishop Laud. He died in 1644.

From Myddfai take the road going west then north-west to Myrtle Hill (767308). Here, go left along the lane to Pont Pwll-defaid (785311). Beyond the bridge go right on a minor road to reach, at 761311, a track heading north. Follow this past Pant y Gaseg Farm, at 761313, to reach Cefn Rhuddan at 762321. Go north again to 763326 where a track goes east to 765326. There it turns north-east for Cefn-yr-allt Uchaf, at 768332. From here a footpath contours around the hill to the mill at 771341, and from there a lane leads to the road for Llanymddyfri (Llandovery. This section of the route, from Myddfai to Llanymddyfri, has some very fine 'soft' scenery, and is a good introduction to the joys to come, as the route heads north from the town to the plateau of Elenydd.

Elenydd

Llanymddyfri (Llandovery)

Llanymddyfri has been important ever since the Roman invasion of Wales, as the site lay at the intersection of several important river valleys; those of the Bran, Tywi and Gwydderig, and thus on the cross-roads of highways between important forts. As a consequence there was a Roman fort here, the earthworks still remaining to the north-east of the town. In the centre of the earthworks is St Mary's Church. Since it cannot now be established as fact, it must be conjecture that the fort had a temple, and that this site was maintained as a holy one after the Romans had retreated and were replaced by early Christians. It is likely therefore that St Mary's is the latest in the line of holy buildings that have occupied the same site for nearly two thousand years. The church has few features remaining of what was probably the earliest stone structure, the Norman building. In the main it is newer, and has suffered much from restoration, though the fourteenth-century tower with its little stair-turret is largely original and very pleasant. In the churchyard is buried one of Llanymddyfri's more famous sons, William Williams, Pantycelyn, the hymn writer, whose statue stands in the Marble Hall of Cardiff's Civic Centre. Williams was born locally in 1717 and after being, briefly, a student of medicine, devoted his life to the church, initially as an Anglican curate and later as a Methodist minister. He died in 1791 and is buried on the north side of St Mary's beneath a polished red granite obelisk which was erected at a later date. The inscribed name Williams Pantycelyn is from his home, and is the name generally given to him still to this day.

Following the departure of the Romans the site was probably abandoned, at least partially, for when Dingat, son of Prince Brychan, founded a church in the hamlet here in the fifth century it was not on the site of the Roman fort, but to the south-west of the present town centre. Prince Brychan is said to have given his name to Brycheiniog (Breconshire), the area prior to his time being known as Garthmadrun. In appearance St Dingat's is similar to St Mary's, with its squat embattled tower. Its history is more chequered, St Dingat's having been twice ruined by fire in uprisings. Later it was badly flooded, as was much of the town, when Afon Tywi burst its banks in the seventeenth century. Many buildings were destroyed with men and animals drowned. It was said, though not until later, that the graveyard was scoured, with bodies floating away. At the time of the flood there was a man working on the banks having guaranteed, at a price, to prevent any future flooding. Not surprisingly he was conspicuous by his absence, as were his banks, after the waters receded. A more permanent solution was applied later when the river, either of its own accord or with assistance, moved to a more easterly course.

That there are two churches in the town is a curiosity and probably implies that at one stage there were actually two parishes, Llandingat near St Dingat's and Llanymddyfri after St Mary's, the church on the Dyfri as Nant Bawddwr was then known. The latter name was adopted for the town, the former church now being the parish church. The name was also given to the castle that the Normans constructed when they moved into the area. Originally the Normans used the Roman fortification adding a motte that can still be seen – St Mary's Church stands on it – but the site was unsatisfactory as its perimeter was too large to hold successfully with limited soldiers, and so another castle was built to the south. This was taken and retaken in various skirmishes for about 150 years, and then sacked by Owain Glyndŵr. Now only the remnants of the keep remain. These are on private land owned by the Castle Hotel, from which permission to view may be obtained.

During the course of the Glyndŵr revolt the town saw some of the brutality of the conflict at first hand. As mentioned earlier Glyndŵr sacked the castle, but that was after Henry IV had used it on his first march into Wales in 1400. As an early attempt to stop the revolt getting out of hand, Henry had one Llywelyn ap Gruffudd Fychan, a local landowner, hanged, drawn and quartered in the market square. His crime was that his sons were believed to be with Owain. Since Owain's sacking of the castle also included the firing of the town and the killing of some inhabitants, the Llanymddyfri townsfolk must have felt that a third opinion was what was required. Less than one hundred years later, another local was in trouble with the English Royal House. This time it was the lord, Rhys ap Gruffudd – or Rhys fitz Urien as he liked to be called, believing himself to be descended from Urien, a knight of King Arthur. Rhys was a champion of Katherine of Aragon in her fight to avoid divorce, and thus did not endear himself to Anne Boleyn. Once in power she persuaded Henry VIII that Rhys's love of the name Urien concealed a love of the name Arthur, Henry's brother, meaning a dislike of Henry and a desire for Welsh sovereignty. This is tortured logic by any standards but it worked, and Rhys was beheaded for treason.

Following this time of unpleasantness, Llanymddyfri settled down to quiet prosperity assisted by its fairs and twice-weekly markets. This peaceable existence allowed the established religions to flourish. The Nonconformists arrived and held meetings in a local cave, and Rhys Prichard became town vicar. Prichard was a man of absolute piety, forever pointing out the iniquities of his flock, and writing a book of religious verse, *Canwyll y Cymry* (the Welshman's Candle), for which he is renowned. It appears likely that his uncompromising piety and total honesty were the reasons that the story of his drunkenness became rife after his death. It is almost as though the man was so good that folk had to invent a little badness to prevent themselves being blinded by the light. There was a saying among Llanymddyfri folk, according to George Borrow writing nearly 200 years later, that 'bad we may be, but not half as bad as the parson'. But Borrow also noted that Prichard was still known as *The* Vicar. Prichard was buried in St Dingat's churchyard, but the site of his grave is not known.

War having been the problem during Llanymddyfri's early years, it is ironic that it was war that led to a sharp increase in prosperity in the late eighteenth century. The European war was preventing England from receiving meat from the continent and so the driving of Welsh animals to England, a trade that had been established since early times, increased dramatically. The droving trade will be mentioned again farther north when a drove-road is briefly followed. In the trade, Llanymddyfri was of considerable importance.

It was a large town, by the standards of the day, with many inns. It was strategically placed at fords and valley heads, and to help overcome the problem of robbery, a Llanymddyfri man set up one of the first banks. This was the Black Ox Bank, the Ox appearing on receipts and cheques, and made the town very popular with those drovers anxious to retain some of their cash. The droving business provided prosperity not only to the innkeepers, but to a host of townsfolk whose trade depended on the cattle: the skinners and leather-tanners, the saddlers and glove-makers.

The same geographical factors that led to Llanymddyfri's importance as a droving station also led to its becoming a coaching station. The prosperity derived from droving and coaching continued when the railway put an end to both trades because Llanymddyfri's position meant it was still important as a meeting and market town, and since a railway station was placed here, what it lost on one hand it gained on the other. The prosperity is reflected in the architecture of the town with its collection of late Georgian buildings. Especially fine is the town hall completed in 1858, and incorporating an open market hall at one end. It is an imposing structure which is the fourth in a line of halls on the site. The immediate predecessor of this hall was a building somewhat lacking in charm if the records are to be believed, for it was not only a crumbling ruin but required the town council to pay 2s. 6d. to Ebenezer Thomas, the butcher, for the occasional use of his dog to kill rats. Elsewhere in the square, the King's Head and the original Market Hall with its clock tower are worthy of note, and other houses in Broad Street and High Street make a quiet walk around the town very worthwhile.

Gone now are the days of the early nineteenth century when visitors to Llanymddyfri found it less than endearing. Malkin found 'its buildings are mean, irregular and unconnected; its streets filthy and disgusting', and a little later someone thought the town had 'nothing to recommend it . . . a few straggling streets generally extremely dirty'. But when George Borrow came fifty years later he was enchanted. On leaving he wrote, 'I have no hesitation in saying (Llanymddyfri) is above the pleasantest little town in which I have halted in the course of my wanderings'.

Llanymddyfri to Rhandir-mwyn

Unfortunately we too must leave Llanymddyfri. The route followed depends as much upon the wayfarer's method of accommodation as upon anything else at this stage. Youth hostellers making for the hostel east of Rhandir-mwyn may go along the minor road that leaves the A483 at 771354 going north via 783407 and 783419 for Hafod-y-pant (800432) where the warden lives. It is obviously a matter of choice but the route that follows the lanes from 761348 or 767347 along the Tywi valley towards Rhandir-mwyn seems preferable, as it offers very fine views up the valley. A visit may be made to Cil-y-cwm, which is a picturesque village with cobbled edges to its street, grouped around a fine fifteenth-century church restored with taste in the early 1900s, and containing an original family box pew. There are also several Non-conformist chapels, including a tiny Baptist chapel in keeping with the compact nature of this delightful spot.

It is to Rhandir-mwyn, however, that the wayfarer is

travelling and the history of the area around the village comes as a great surprise. Despite the image that Wales, other than the valleys, now conveys, of a largely agricultural-based country, historically the country has always been important industrially. This is largely due to its enormous mineral wealth. Lately this has meant slate and coal, but in earlier days, when industry was on a more piecemeal basis and production was limited, it also meant metal mining. At times when the need for expensive metals, and even iron, was small, Wales was a prospector's paradise. There were lead mines in every one of the old Welsh counties, gold in Caerfyrddin and Meirionnydd, most particularly in the area around Dolgellau; and copper in Môn (Anglesey) and Caernarfon, with Mynydd Parys in Môn being a famous site.

The largest mine in Caerfyrddin, indeed in the whole of South Wales, was here at Rhandir-mwyn. Indeed the name means mining district, the site itself being called Nantymwyn from the position of the main shafts on the banks of Nant y Bai, which drains the hills to the south of Llyn Brianne down into Afon Tywi. The mining was spread over a wide area, as it occurred over a long period, and the wayfarer coming upon the remains suddenly is somewhat taken aback by the sight of industrial spoil in this, one of the most peaceful and secluded valleys in the whole of Wales. It is difficult to be precise about dates in some of the Welsh mines as it is possible that minor workings existed by Roman times, but by 1775 the mine was being worked in earnest, and very profitably. A fine watercolour by Warwick Smith, now in the National Library of Wales, Aberystwyth, shows the surface workings of the mine in 1792, as dated, with a large water-wheel beside a small number of buildings. It is likely that the water-wheel was the source of power in an ore-crushing house, the remains of a stack indicating that at a later stage the wheel was replaced by a steam engine. As much as 4,000 tons of ore were raised annually at the time of highest output. The site was never served by tram

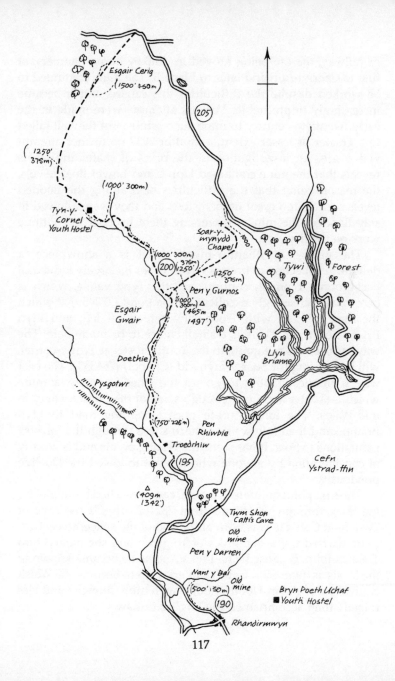

Esgair Cerig
(1500' 450m)

(205)

(1250' 375m)

(1000' 300m)

Ty'n-y-Cornel Youth Hostel

Soar-y-mynydd Chapel

Tywi Forest

(1000' 300m)

(200) 375m (1250')

(1250' 375m)

Pen y Gurnos

(1000' 300m) △ 465m (1497')

Esgair Gwair

Doethie

Llyn Brianne

Pysgotwr

(750' 225m)

Pen Rhiwbie

Troedrhiw

(195)

Cefn Ystrad-ffin

△ (409m 1342')

Twm Shon Catti's Cave

Old mine

Pen y Darren

Nant y Bai

Old mine

(500' 50m)

(190)

Bryn Poeth Uchaf
■ Youth Hostel

Rhandirmwyn

117

or railway, the ore being moved in donkey-borne panniers, at first to Caerfyrddin and later to Llanelli. The mine continued to be worked despite the difficulties this caused, but it became increasingly unprofitable. Various attempts were made in the early twentieth century to mine successfully, but they all failed to a greater or lesser extent, and after 1937 no further attempt was made. An investigation of the plans of shafts and levels reveals that the mine contained Upper and Lower Boat Levels, the reason being that the difficulties of draining the flooded levels became too great on occasions and they were allowed to stay flooded, the miners traversing them by boat to continue work on the dry side.

The village of Rhandir-mwyn itself is a showpiece, a delightful collection of houses which belies its largely industrial background. From it, continue up the Tywi valley, which is becoming increasingly excellent, to the point (772459) at which the road divides, with Troed-rhiw signed off left, and Llyn Brianne off right. There is a small choice to be made here. The wayfarer, if he is not going to the Youth Hostel at Ty'n-y-cornel, will be heading for Soar-y-mynydd (Chapel) (784533). The best way is unquestionably to go up the Doethie valley, a route which is shorter and goes through some of the finest scenery in mid-Wales. The longer route goes along the road to Llyn Brianne and then follows its eastern shore through the forestry plantations to Soar. It has some interesting points and is worthy of consideration by anyone who has not followed the Doethie previously.

The first point of interest, a cave, can be reached by following the track through woodland from 782463. This is the cave of Twm Siôn Cati. He was born at the end of the sixteenth century to unmarried Catherine Jones of Tregaron and she named him Thomas John. Because he had no surname he became known to the locals as Twm Siôn Cati. Twm grew up to become the Welsh equivalent of Robin Hood, though with more humour and less tragedy than accompanied the English outlaw.

Continuing along the road the wayfarer reaches Llyn Brianne. This is an artificial lake, a reservoir behind a thoroughly modern dam that is nearly 90m high. The flooding of the area was, at the time, a tragedy, but there is no denying the beauty that has been created by the lake. At the base of the dam is a flip-bucket' water discharge which causes a fountain of water (of the same appearance, but considerably bigger, than those that hold up golf balls at fun fairs) that sparkles in the sun causing its own rainbow. The water authority, sensing that many will find the dam wall, flip bucket and lake attractive, has carefully stage-managed the area, with car parks and viewing points.

The way to Soar-y-mynydd is now a straightforward and pleasant, if long, trek through the woodland of Tywi forest, around the shores of the lake.

The better route takes the road to Troed-rhiw, a road that follows one bank and then the other of the Doethie river. This is delightful country, one of the very best valleys in mid-Wales with good views all around. Indeed, this entire section from south of Rhandir-mwyn, approaching the head of the Tywi valley and then taking the narrow valley of a tributary, is one of the better lowland sections on the whole journey from Cardiff to Conwy. In its early stages the road passes between the RSPB reserves of Dinas, to the right, and Gwenffrwd, to the left.

The road we are on now is an old drove-road and it would be good to think that the drovers chose this way as much for its aesthetic qualities as for its speed. The drovers performed from the Middle Ages onwards the job that brought fame to the cowboys of the mid-west of America in the nineteenth century. The first drovers were probably pre-Norman, but it became an established practice in Norman times and continued until the nineteenth century when better transport brought the trade to an end. The herds were generally taken over the barren mountain ways so that the crop-lands were not interfered with, and their progress can occasionally be noted by the siting of a

Butcher's Arms, animals being slaughtered en route to provide local meat supplies. Unlike the US mid-west droves, it was not only cattle that came. Then, as now, the sheep was the chief animal of upland Wales, but there were also pigs and geese and later turkeys as well. A large drove must have been a spectacular sight. Together with the animals were the drovers, of course, and many other travellers, for Wales was a wild place and there was safety in numbers. The drovers worked hard on the big herds and relaxed on the way back, taking a coach perhaps and the occasional night at an inn. If they managed to avoid being robbed they probably arrived back broke, and just in time to drive again.

We travel in the footsteps, or should it be hoof-marks, of the drovers and their herds back up the Doethie valley to 771514 where paths go on up the valley to Ty'n-y-cornel, and right (the drove-road) to Soar-y-mynydd chapel. Youth hostellers carrying on here need not, in fact, visit the chapel as they may receive permission at the hostel to move northwards to reach the mountain road at 762576. The right of way goes right to Soar-y-mynydd, the loneliest chapel in Wales to which worshippers came on horse-back, and from there by lane – it is hardly a road – to the same point. From here the true Elenydd is crossed.

Elenydd

The name Elenydd is an ancient one. Giraldus Cambrensis uses it to describe the whole of the mountain area of South Wales, as opposed to Eryri, the mountains of North Wales. However, since Giraldus used the name Pumlumon, and recognised the sandstone masses of what is now the Brecon Beacons National Park, he clearly meant by Elenydd that area between Pumlumon and Mynydd Du. Giraldus claims the area was called, in English, Moruge, though there appears little justification for such a claim. It is likely that the name derives from Afon Elan to the north of the area, but it is such a delightful name that it seems fitting to apply it to the entire high plateau area north of the Tywi valley and Rhandir-mwyn, and south of the Wye valley and Pumlumon. The eastern part of this area is the Welsh lake district, a series of reservoirs having been created by the damming of the rivers that flowed in the wide valleys. The first, as we have seen, is Llyn Brianne. To the north are the Claerwen and then the reservoirs of the Elan valley. It is an arguable point whether Welsh valleys should be flooded to provide the industrial Midlands of England with water, and any extension of the reservoirs should be viewed cautiously, at least. Since the Elan valley dams were completed in the early years of this century and the Claerwen in the early 1950s the author can claim, by reason of age, to be only capable of assessing the reservoirs as they are, not by a comparison with the unflooded valleys. In that context the water is attractive at a distance, but somewhat sterile, the lack of tree cover at the edges of Claerwen and Craig Goch meaning that the reservoirs do not have the secretive, cool beauty of Llyn Efyrnwy (Lake Vyrnwy) to the north, or even Llyn Brianne for that matter.

However, the suggested route stays to the west of the big reservoirs, visiting instead small pools that are dark and forbidding, and generate a considerable atmosphere. The pools lie above Ystrad Fflur (Strata Florida), and from Rhandir-mwyn there are fifteen miles of quite magnificent moorland to be crossed. The wilderness lover could hardly be better served, the lover of scenic beauty could hardly improve on the valleys of Gwenffrwd, Pysgotwr and Doethie, and for the nature lover there is the red kite. The kite is the most famous and sought-after of Welsh raptors, though it is probable that the goshawk of Snowdonia, the hen harrier and even, perhaps, the peregrine falcon are rarer. But with its beautiful chestnut colour and deeply forked tail it is one of the finest of British birds. Though the bird is a moorland feeder it nests in trees, and the wooded valleys of north of Rhandir-mwyn are potential nest sites. The bird is a nervous nester and any disturbance can cause it to desert its eggs or chicks. The loss of a brood would be a disaster, and the pestering of the bird at nest cannot be tolerated. It is likely that the wayfarer will take two days to reach Cwmystwyth. During the whole of that time he may see the bird working the ridges on the moor, so there is no need to go searching for it.

Our route leads northwards across the moorland. This section is a very real test of navigational ability, and the wayfarer should consider very carefully before embarking on a crossing if the weather is poor and visibility limited. The route starts easily enough along the track to Nant-y-maen (761585), but beyond that there is no real path and the ground can be marshy, particularly in wet weather. In good weather or, rather, in good visibility, this section of the route, and that to the north of Ystrad Fflur over similar terrain, are very fine, even beautiful if the walker's idea of beauty extends to weather-beaten moorland offering, at best, solitude, at worst loneliness. There are no real landmarks, but the top of Garn Gron (740611) can be a haven to the traveller who is a little bewildered. It must be borne in mind, however, that the summit is actually right in the middle of nowhere. North of Garn Gron the walker goes west of the crags of Carn Fflur (743625) to discover that there is now forestry down to grid line 63. This does nothing to improve the navigation, indeed far from it because the trees cut down the view considerably. But wayfarers are assisted by blue waymarkers which guide them through the forest (the work of Tony Drake) to Talwrn (745649), a dangerous ruin, but useful landmark. From it an obvious path leads down to the abbey of Ystrad Fflur (Strata Florida) (746657), the latter part of which involves crossing a stream several times.

Ystrad Fflur (Strata Florida)

The remains of Strata Florida are not extensive but the pastoral setting, on the banks of Afon Teifi, is wonderfully peaceful. Strangely the name derives not from the river, the name being the Latin form of Ystrad Fflur, the valley of Afon Fflur that also

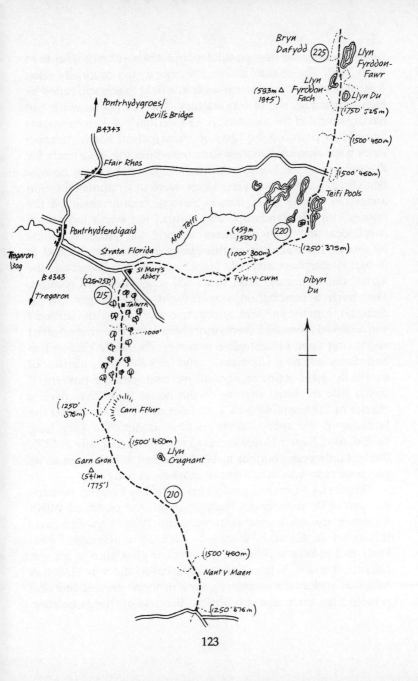

Bryn
Dafydd (225)

Llyn
Fyrddon-
Fawr

(593m △
1945')

Llyn
Fyrddon-
Fach

Llyn Du

(1750' 525m)

Pontrhydygroes/
Devil's Bridge

↑

B4343

(1500' 450m)

Ffair Rhos

(1500' 460m)

Teifi Pools

Afon Teifi

(459m
1500') (220)

Pontrhydfendigaid

Strata Florida (1000' 300m) (1250' 375m)

Tregaron
30g

B4343 St Mary's
Abbey

↓
Tregaron (225m750') Ty'n-y-cwm Dibyn
Du

(215)

Talwrn

-1000'

(1250'
376m) Carn Fflur

(1500' 450m)

Garn Gron
△
(541m
1775')

Llyn
Crugnant

(210)

(1500' 460m)

Nant y Maen

(1250' 876m)

123

runs into Tregaron Bog, parallel to, but 3.5kms (2 miles) south of Afon Teifi. The reason is that the abbey was originally sited 3.5kms (2 miles) to the south-west in a field that is still called Yr Hen Fynachlog, the old monastery. The Normans, while not having invented the monastic house, certainly did an enormous amount to promote the idea of monasticism. Many Norman lords gave land and money for house-building, and lands for the upkeep of the house and monks. All of the great houses, Benedictine, Cistercian, Franciscan, were of Continental origin and while the English, that is Saxons, readily absorbed the houses into their landscape and culture, the Welsh were more suspicious: the foreign houses seemed too attached to the Normans. The founding of this abbey is generally ascribed to Robert FitzStephen who held large tracts of West Wales, and the agreed date is around 1160, some 100 years after the Conquest. That such a benefaction was fraught with danger can be deduced from the fact that, within two years, Rhys ap Gruffudd had attacked Norman Ceredigion, conquering the whole district and taking Robert FitzStephen prisoner. The house FitzStephen had founded was Cistercian, and extolled the virtues of simplicity, hard work in agriculture, and extreme poverty. It seems that the quiet dignity of the house won Rhys over, a charter of 1184 naming him as builder of the abbey. In fact the building of the abbey seems to have occupied a very long period, the Chapter House having been completed only in 1235, the bell only being bought in 1254. The bell is of interest as its purchase price was ninety-seven marks and two cows.

Despite its Norman foundations the abbey became, perhaps because of its remoteness from England, the centre of Welsh influence, and also a great cultural centre. When Llywelyn Fawr (Llywelyn the Great) of Gwynedd decided to assemble Welsh lords and princes together to swear their allegiance to his son Dafydd, it was to Ystrad Fflur that he called them in 1238. It is said that within the cemetery many of these princes and also princes from later ages are buried. Because of this association with Welsh nationalism, the abbey has been called the Welsh Westminster. It fared badly in the rebellion of Owain Glyndŵr, for in 1401 when the army of Henry IV was being harried by the guerrilla fighters of the Welsh prince a baggage train belonging to his young son, Henry, Prince of Wales, was attacked and robbed. King Henry was furious and marched on Strata Florida. There, he and his knights released the pent-up frustrations of the failing Welsh campaign in a blasphemous fury. The abbey was plundered, its holy vessels stolen, its buildings looted, and many monks were murdered. Henry ordered that the horses should be tethered at the high altar, with inevitable consequences for the church. His knights drank the abbey's wine cellars dry in a two-day spree, then smashed down the buildings and fired the ruins. In later life Henry is reported to have been in an agony of conscience over the acts, though this must have been much later as his son quartered an army here in 1407 during the siege of Aberystwyth castle. The holiness of the spot meant that when peace returned the abbey was rebuilt, and was in constant occupation up until the time of dissolution.

Despite the ravages suffered by the abbey in the early fifteenth century, and a fire following a lightning strike in the late thirteenth century, there is a considerable amount of Norman work in the abbey including a superb Norman doorway. Not much else of the structure remains intact. Following dissolution the abbeys were customarily stripped of their roofs and over a period of time the walls collapsed, a decay assisted by locals who used the abbeys (and castles) as a convenient quarry for building stone. As a consequence little remains that is immediately discernible to the layman. Nevertheless the site still has a quiet dignity.

As mentioned before, the abbey cemetery is the burial place of many of the early princes of the territories of Wales. The church cemetery beside it was the burial place of Dafydd ap Gwilym, the greatest of medieval Welsh poets who was buried here in the latter part of the fourteenth century. Traditionally

Dafydd was buried under the yew tree, though the memorials to him are very recent. He was born at Penrhyncoch near Aberystwyth and is renowned for his prose poems on all subjects from love to humour. He is especially fine at describing the natural world. His liking for humour suggest that Dafydd would have liked the memorial erected near his yew tree in 1756. The tombstone was incised with a leg to the thigh, the inscription reading 'The leg and part of the thigh of Henry Hughes, Cooper, was cut off and interred here June 18th 1756'. Hughes was injured in a stage coach crash, but survived and prospered well enough to emigrate to the USA on his one leg.

Ystrad Fflur to Cwmystwyth

From the abbey ruins take the lane going eastward to Ty'n-y-cwm Farm (771655) from where a path leads back onto the moorland of Elenydd. To the north-east from here are the Teifi pools (Llyn Teifi) close to which is some of the wildest and loneliest, but at the same time loveliest, country of Elenydd. The land here is grassland, one of the few remaining areas in Wales of grass moor, as opposed to rough or peat moor, left unpolluted by ranks of conifers. It is a land of great beauty with a flora that could keep the most difficult to please flower-lover busy for some time, and gives again the chance of seeing kites. The pools feed Afon Teifi that then flows into Cors Tregaron (Tregaron Bog), a grade 1 natural site where many rare bog plants grow and insects abound, and where, in winter, the ducks attract a fine assortment of raptors including the hen harrier. In summer the great grey shrike makes an occasional visit.

The Teifi pools were the scene, in 1929, of a tragedy when an old tramp who had left Ffair-rhos was caught in a blizzard. Then, as now, this was a place of little shelter, and he died of cold and exposure. Not until the snow cleared several weeks later was the body discovered. A search of his body for some identification revealed 8½d, but no name. The farmers and villagers of Ffair-rhos were troubled by the sadness of the incident and money was found for a burial at Ystrad Fflur. On a slab stone a local carved the epitaph –

UNKNOWN
He died upon the hillside drear
Alone where snow was deep
By strangers he was carried here
Where princes also sleep.

It is a sobering thought, particularly if the mist comes down and the temperature drops.

There is now an escape road to Ffair-rhos to the west and, though longer, to Claerwen to the east. Ahead is a 5-mile stretch of relatively featureless moorland, the sensible route to Cwmystwyth being to head off to the Fyrddon lakes, to follow them and then to go north. Strictly this route is not on a right of way, but public access was guaranteed at the time Birmingham Water Works was granted permission to create reservoirs in the Elan valley to the east. The old mining ruins east of Cwmystwyth are worth visiting and can be reached directly by the intrepid stream-crosser or by the bridges, one at Cwmystwyth itself, and one farther east.

Cwmystwyth

Cwmystwyth represents perhaps the most tangible sign of old Ceredigion's (Cardiganshire) mineral wealth, the deserted mine buildings and spoil heaps littering the valley of Afon Ystwyth for several hundred metres. It is a paradise for the mining historian and industrial archaeologist, but even for the casual visitor it is a powerful site. While on the one hand, and from the aesthetic point of view, the site is a desolation, a vandalising of a beautiful river valley, and a dangerous vandalism at that, on the other hand the creaking doors, the wind in the old buildings, and the ghosts of past presences lend an air of mystery and a link with a richer lode of life. Despite the ruins, the site is an empty and lonely one, and the wayfarer who visits alone and wanders through it will experience an isolation which does not exist to the same intensity on the lonely moorland to the south.

It was noted, in 1872, that the mine was 'both the richest and the oldest wrought mine in the county (of Ceredigion), having produced considerably more than two million sterling of lead ore'. That is an enormous financial profit, and represents, in ore terms, the mining of, probably, in excess of 100,000 tons of rock. The reasons for the richness is that the site is above not one, but a dozen or so lodes, not only of lead, but also of copper. The area has certainly been worked since earliest times as stone tools have been found on Copper Hill to the east of the main workings. The name is interesting as it appears to have been given to the hill quite specifically, but is entered on the Ordnance Survey maps as Copa Hill. Since 'copa' is Welsh for crest, or top, a term which could only marginally be applied to the hill, and not for copper, it is perhaps an example of an English name 'Welshised' as opposed to a Welsh one Anglicised. The hill was later mined by the scouring technique applied, as we have seen, to expose coal and ironstone at Blaenafon. Here the technique was called hushing and has produced a series of radiating gashes from an old reservoir on the hill above Nant yr Onnen (stream). It is believed by many experts to represent the finest example of the technique in Britain, though in purely aesthetic terms it can hardly be said to enhance the beauty of the valley of the small stream.

The earliest workings of the lodes were by the cutting of open trenches or by the boring of adits. An adit was a shaft that entered the hillside horizontally or, in practice, sloping upwards slightly, so that water collecting at the mining point drained away naturally. Drainage was a problem which was always encountered in Welsh mineral mines, and is of course a problem of mines generally. Before the invention of the water pump, or any successful method of powering such a pump over the large distances required, inclined adits represented the simplest

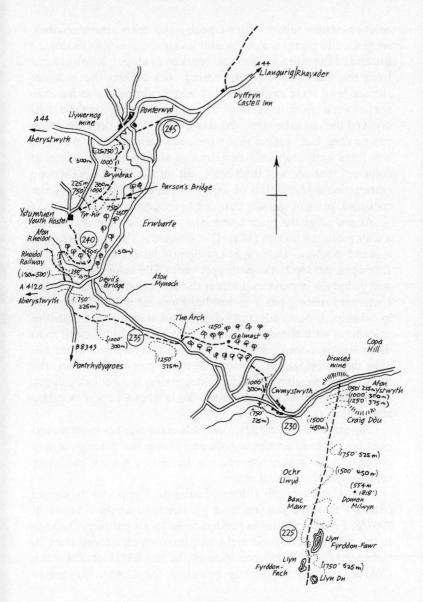

A 44
Llangurig/Rhayader

Dyffryn
Castell Inn

Ponterwyd

Llywernog
mine

A 44
Aberystwyth

(245)

(25 750)
(300m)
1000'

225 m   300m
750   1000'

Brynbras

Parson's Bridge

Ystumtuen
Youth Hostel

Tyr-hir

750'
250'

Erwbarfe

Afon
Rheidol

(240)

(500')

150m

Rheidol
Railway

(150m 500')

250'
15 m

A 4120
Aberystwyth

Devil's
Bridge

Afon
Mynach

(750'
225m)

The Arch

1250'

Gelmast

(1000'
300m)

(235)

(1250'
375m)

Copa
Hill

Disused
mine

B 8343

Pontrhydygroes

1006'
300m)

Cwmystwyth

Afon
ystwyth
050' 225m
(1000' 300m)
(1250' 375m)

(750'
225m)

(230)

(1500'
450m)

Craig Ddu

(1750 525 m)

Ochr
Llwyd

(1500' 450 m)

(554m
• 1818')

Banc
Mawr

Domen
Milwyn

(225)

Llyn
Fyrddon-Fawr

Llyn
Fyrddon-
Fach

(1750' 525m)

Llyn Du

129

solution. Later when water-wheels, and then steam engines, were sited to pump water, the adit levels were used as drains. At the end of the adit the lode was worked in stopes, levels cut out from the adit into the ore-bearing rock. When the lodes at surface level were exhausted and water pumping was feasible, shafts were sunk vertically. The adit working method had allowed the ore to be removed straightforwardly, ore carts being run on rails, but vertical shafts required hand or horse powered windings and, later, winding frames similar to those used at collieries. The ore was then lifted out in a kibble, a bucket-type carrier. Some separation of metal and metal concentrate from rock took place at the site in order to reduce the carriage.

At one stage the main Cwmystwyth shafts were drained by a water-wheel 9 metres (30 feet) in diameter. The water-wheel is a grand machine, the one at Llywernog farther north being, at 15 metres (50 feet), a superb specimen. The impression of size and grandeur is enhanced when the wheels are set, as was the customary mining practice, not hard against mill buildings but in wheelpits. Not only the wheels, but some of the statistics associated with them, are astonishing, for a 12 metre (40 foot) diameter, over-shot wheel, that is one in which the water ran over the wheel, could produce 25 hp. If run continuously, the daily water requirement was a staggering six million gallons. Such a consumption would lower the level of a 10-acre pond by about 80cm (2.5feet)!

The mine closed in 1921, since when the site has been picked over by visitors, archaeologists and the wind. Though it will never be as it was before mining started, it is very gradually returning to the natural state.

From Cwmystwyth village take the track opposite the chapel (786743) to some houses, and go north to another house at 796748. From here care is needed to follow a pathway through to the road at 783751. Go right and then left on a forest track to Gelmast (776756) and continue on to the B4574 at The Arch (765756) erected in 1810 to celebrate the Golden Jubilee of

George III's accession. Here, go right and then left off the road on a track that leads straightforwardly to the B4343 at 738764. Go right, and down to Pontarfynach (Devil's Bridge).

Pontarfynach (Devil's Bridge)

Here is the first of the 'honeypots' that the wayfarer meets on his journey northward. There will be others and the traveller should think deeply before shunning such spots. There is much here that is truly delightful, even if some of it is enclosed by wire and visited only by those who pay. The system calls to mind the story of the traveller in America who stayed at a hotel close to a particularly beautiful gorge. A pathway to, and a viewpoint of, the scene had been beaten to the spot and there the visitor was confronted by a sign that read 'View by kind permission of – Hotel' to which someone had added 'with just a little help from God'.

The river at this point is Afon Mynach, as the abbey of Ystrad Fflur owned sheep grazing lands in the area. It was the monks from Ystrad Fflur who built the first, and lowest (of course!), of the bridges over the ravine. This bridge was built in 1087, and looks as usable now, in theory only, as it was nine hundred years ago. The bridge also gave the spot its true name, Pontarfynach. The name Devil's Bridge is derived from the Welsh Pont y Gŵr Drwg (roughly the bridge of the evil one), which is from a legend regarding the establishment of the first bridge. The legend concerns Marged, an old woman who lived in a cottage close to the edge of the ravine. Marged's sole source of income was her cow, Malen, whom she milked daily, selling the milk to her neighbours. One morning Marged went out to milk Malen after a night of particularly heavy rain to discover that the cow has crossed the river above the ravine and was now marooned on the far side by the raging torrent. Marged was beside herself as not milking Malen would not only mean no money, but also that the cow would suffer. Standing at the edge of the ravine she called out in despair that she would give anything for a bridge

131

to cross it. Immediately a voice answered saying that he would build her a bridge, and looking up Marged saw a figure in the white habit and cowl of an Ystrad Fflur Cistercian monk on the far side. The cowl over his head seemed curiously shaped and he was turned so that his face did not show, but despite this, and the fact that she could hear him clearly over the roar of the water, Marged was so heartened that she asked how long it might take. Just an hour, said the monk, provided that he was allowed to take the first living thing that crossed it. In her excitement Marged took little notice of his final proviso and hurried back to her cottage, the monk having told her that she must not witness the miraculous bridge building. At the cottage she ate a hurried breakfast and at last she heard the monk's voice calling her. She rushed back to the ravine still holding a bread crust, and accompanied by her dog. There was indeed a bridge across the ravine and on the far side was the monk holding Malen. Marged started to cross but at that instant the monk's cowl slipped slightly and Marged saw that its curious shape was due to the monk having horns. Instantly she realised that it was the Devil in disguise, and that he was after her soul.

She was a wily old lady, however, and so she hesitated, staring at the bridge. The Devil, impatient for her soul, asked why. She replied that the bridge did not seem strong enough to carry her crust of bread let alone herself. The Devil told her to throw it on to the bridge to see, if she felt that way, but instead Marged threw the crust right across the bridge and her dog immediately followed it, becoming the first living thing to cross. Furious, the Devil disappeared in a cloud of sulphurous smoke leaving Marged to cross the bridge and to be re-untied with both Malen and the dog.

The triple bridge structure gives some idea of the advance of bridge-building techniques. As the span length increased, so the bridge moved up towards the top of the ravine. The second bridge was built over the first in 1708, while the top bridge is modern. Beneath the bridges are the Mynach Falls and the

Devil's Punchbowl, for which the site is so justly renowned. The Punchbowl is an elegantly smooth hollow carved from the mountainside by the river. To the north of the bridges a pathway descends 90 metres (300 feet) on the eastern side of the river, crosses it and follows it closely on the ascent side to view the magnificent falls themselves. The path involves a steep section known, with little imagination, as Jacob's Ladder, which has been known to stop the elderly. At the top of the climb is the Hafod Arms Hotel, the 'immense lofty cottage with projecting eaves' where George Borrow stayed when visiting the gorge. Borrow described the scene with the awe-struck horror that seemed to be the requirement of visitors of the period. The Punchbowl becomes 'a frightful cavity (where) the waters . . . whirl, boil and hiss in a horrid pot or cauldron . . . in a manner truly tremendous'. The waters then escape through 'a gloomy volcanic slit'. Borrow suggested that after seeing the Punchbowl, not the name he used as he called it by the local name of Twll yn y Graig, the hole in the cliff, and the 'spectral, shadowy Devil's Bridge', you should 'repair to your inn, and have no more sight-seeing that day, for you have seen enough!' Neither would he come to terms with the falls themselves which 'is thundering beside you; foam, foam, foam is flying all about you; the basin . . . is boiling frightfully below you', together with 'rocks . . . frowning terribly on you' and 'forest trees, dank and wet with spray and mist'. It would be interesting to find out if Borrow really did find it so bad, or whether the time (he was in Wales around 1855) and his intended audience coloured his perception. For the modern wayfarer it is all of these horrid, frightful things that are so attractive, and he can handle them in quantities in excess of one per day.

Interestingly Borrow does not mention the legend of Marged and the Devil, but he does mention a story centred on a cave, now no longer visible as such, at the base of the falls. Here, he says, lived the Plant de Bat (or children of Bat), a local man. These, two boys and a girl, were notorious locally as petty thieves. One day they killed a gentleman while robbing him, and his friends sought them out, destroying the cave so they could no longer use it. The boys were hanged and the girl burnt at the stake.

To continue from Pontarfynach, go west along the A4120 to reach a path leading off right (north) at 735770. Follow this to, alongside, then across (and across again) the railway. This is the Vale of Rheidol railway, the only steam railway operated by British Rail in the days before privatisation. It runs from Aberystwyth to the terminus at Pontarfynach. Though not, perhaps, having the charm of the Festiniog railway, nor the dramatic impact of the Tal-y-llyn railway at Abergynolwyn, the Rheidol is a fine track, arguably better than the other 'Great Little Trains'. The Rheidol is a fine valley and is well seen on this short walk along it. The path drops down to the river, crossing it by a bridge. Now head north to reach a better defined path which leads to the Ystumtuen Youth Hostel.

The wayfarer is now seeking to reach Dyffryn Castell for access to Pumlumon. From Ystumtuen, follow the road to Tŷ Hir (738789), from where a waymarked path heads east to Parson's Bridge, a new footbridge over a superb gorge. Beyond the bridge is a very ancient church which had no resident vicar, one riding up the Rheidol from Aberystwyth to take services. As the original bridge was only a plank he tied his mount here, at the parson's bridge. The church is set near some ancient standing stones. This has led some to believe that it was deliberately set up within a henge site that may have had some contemporary pagan significance. The wayfarer can now follow the main road towards Ponterwyd, or alternatively, continue along the road north of Tŷ Hir: the road becomes unfenced allowing access to Bryn Bras. Head north to reach a path which is followed through fields to a footbridge (at 745804) and on to the George Borrow Hotel at Ponterwyd.

To the left at this point the wayfarer can visit another mining site, but this time not a site of great importance or great atmosphere. In fact the Llywernog lead mine was somewhat insignificant in actual mining terms, but it has now been turned into a spectacular museum of the industry. There are several water-wheels on site, complete specimens having been brought in to augment the site wheel. Close to one of the wheels are a pair of round buddles, sedimentation pools for the recovery of fine particles of lead that had escaped from the jiggers. The jiggers were a series of washing tubs in which the heavy lead-ore sank away from the lighter waste. The jiggers are here also, housed in the jigger shed. It is one of the joys of the history of mining that so many words like buddle and jigger were used. In addition, the visitor can walk into the Pumlumon range as far as a pool that is, in fact, a water-filled shaft, the shaft having been driven at the end of the nineteenth century.

Whichever route is used, the wayfarer must reach 752807 (on the main road to Pontarfynach) where a path heads east to the B4343 which is followed to Dyffryn Castell. The lane beside the inn is taken out on to Pumlumon.

Pumlumon

In the Mabinogion the Welsh Arthurian knights Cai and Bedwyr (Kay and Bedivere) are one day 'sitting on Pumlumon, in the greatest wind in the world'. Later another traveller visited the spot and declared it a 'sodden weariness'. Accept the truth of either, or more especially of both, statements, and you would be disinclined to visit at all. You would be wrong. It may be a huge mass rather than a shapely group of peaks, but Pumlumon is still a fine place with excellent walking. The first syllable is certainly from 'pump', five, but what of the rest? There is no clear-cut answer; it could be from five rivers as five at least can be counted, but it is more likely to mean five peaks for, with a little imagination, there can be distinguished five tops around Llyn Llygad Rheidol. The summit of Pen Pumlumon Fawr, the highest peak, just fails to make 2,500ft (762m) which is sad, but what it lacks in inches it makes up for in other ways as it is well protected by bogs and difficult ground, and affords, from its summit, fine views of the route to date over Elenydd and of delights to come, as well as a very fine view of the spidery Nant-y-moch reservoir not so very far below. Almost due east of the summit, and about 1.25km (0.75 mile) away, is the source of Afon Gwy (the River Wye), while a few kilometres north-east is Blaenhafren, the source of the Severn, which is Afon Hafren.

To continue, descend north from the summit to the 'standing stones' marked on the map at 783895. Two stones were said to have been set up to mark the site of the first battle fought by Owain Glyndŵr in his bid to restore Wales's independence from England, and two are shown by the Ordnance Survey, though the single white slab appears unnatural here. Glyndŵr's campaign will be dealt with in greater depth when we reach his capital at Machynlleth, but the battle is worthy of note. In 1401 Glyndŵr had amassed a small army of about four hundred men here in the Hyddgen valley. At the time there was, in South Wales, a strong Flemish community whose lifestyle and affluence depended on English support. They were concerned that the revolt should be nipped in the bud and sent men to support a small English force. This army, about 1,500 strong, found the Welsh in this secluded valley, surrounded them and poured in on to them. Robert Vaughan, a contemporary, wrote of the battle – 'They hemmed him (Glyndŵr) in on all sides so that he could not possibly get off without fighting at a great disadvantage. He and his men fought manfully a great while, in their own defence, against them. Finding themselves surrounded and hard put to it, they resolved at length to make their way through or perish in the attempt; so, falling on furiously, with courage whetted with despair they put the enemy, after a sharp dispute, to confusion; and they pursued so eagerly their advantage, that they bade them give ground, and in the end to fly outright, leaving two hundred of their men dead on the spot of the engagement. This victory rendered Owain considerable renown and was the means to bring many

136

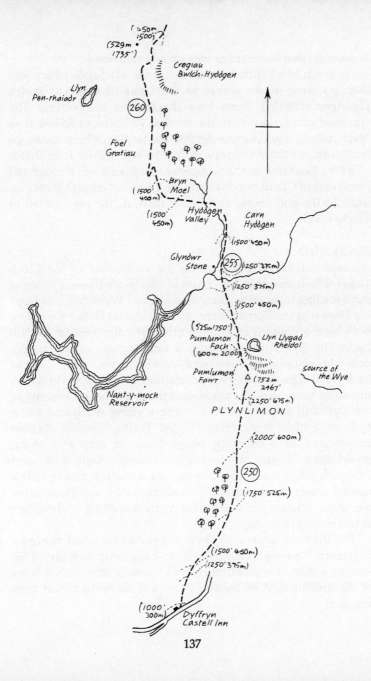

(450m 1500')

(529m 1735')

Llyn Pen-rhaiadr

Cregiau Bwlch-Hyddgen

(260)

Foel Grafiau

Bryn Moel

(1500' 450m)

(1500' 450m)

Hyddgen Valley

Carn Hyddgen

(1500' 450m)

Glyndwr Stone

(255)

(1250' 375m)

(1250' 375m)

(1500' 450m)

(525m 1750')

Pumlumon Fach

(600m 2000')

Llyn Llygad Rheidol

source of the Wye

Nant-y-moch Reservoir

Pumlumon Fawr

△ (752 m 2467')

PLYNLIMON

(2250' 675m)

(2000' 600m)

(250)

(1750' 525m)

(1500' 450m)

(1250' 375m)

(1000' 300m)

Dyffryn Castell Inn

137

to his side, that his number was greatly increased'.

To reach Machynlleth continue up the Hyddgen valley and then go west of the forest to the head of Creigiau Bwlch Hyddgen (766935). From here the choices are endless. The wayfarer can go down to the road at 775960 and follow it to Machynlleth, a good route despite the tarmac. Alternatively go northward to the bridleway at 766956 and follow it to Bwlch (755975). Continue on the bridleway that goes north through the forest east of Glanmerin lake and, at the wood edge (757994), go north to the golf course and minor road. At the road go left to Machynlleth.

Machynlleth

A couple of kilometres or so to the south-west of the Clock Tower which stands in the centre of Machynlleth are a series of steps leading to an area of common land on Wylfa hill. The steps are known as the Roman Steps, as local legend claims they were built by the Romans as access to their frontier post on the hill itself. The legend also includes a further post at Bryn-y-gog, now a housing estate in the north-eastern corner of the town, to back up the known Roman occupation of a fort at Pennal. A thousand years later the position of the town, near a crossing of the Dyfi and at the mouths of valleys going north and south both of which carry rivers called Dulas, gave it distinct advantages as a meeting place. Since it was also about equidistant from other major towns, Dolgellau and Aberystwyth, it was a logical place for a market, and in 1291 a market charter was granted. The allotted day was Wednesday and even now a street market set up by travelling stall-holders is still held on that day.

It is the association with Owain Glyndŵr for which the town is famous however. Glyndŵr is an enigmatic man in Welsh history, a man of sophistication and learning, and with dreams of the greatness of Wales as a culturally separate nation from England.

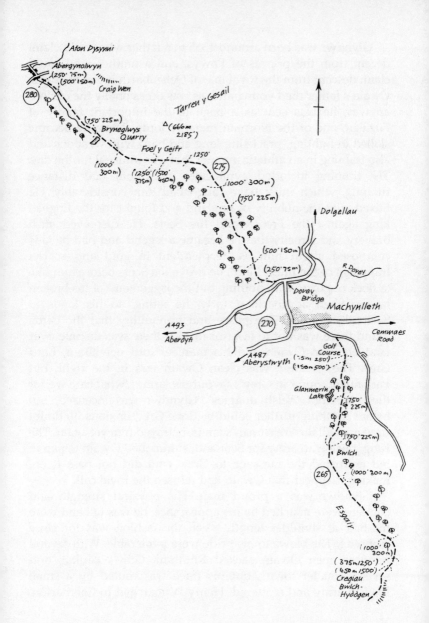

Afon Dysynni

Abergynolwyn
(250' 75m)
(500' 150m)

Craig Wen

280

Tarren y Gesail

(750' 225m)

Bryneglwys Quarry

Foel y Geifr

1250'

(1000' 300m)

(1250' 375m) (1500' 450m)

275

(1000' 300m)

(750' 225m)

Dolgellau

(500' 150m)

(250' 75m)

R. Dovey

Dovey Bridge

Machynlleth

A 493
Aberdyfi

270

Cemmaes Road

A 487
Aberystwyth

Golf Course
('5m 250')
(150m 500')

Glanmerin Lake

(750' 225m)

(750' 225m)

Bwlch

265

(1000' 300m)

Esgair

(1000' 300m)

(375m/250')
(450m 1500')

Cregiau Bwlch-Hyddgen

139

Glyndŵr was born around 1355 to a father who could claim decent from the princes of Powys, and a mother who could claim descent from the royal line of Deheubarth in South Wales. Owain's father died young and, as was occasionally the custom anyway, he was sent as a page to the important family of Fitzalan, one of the Norman marcher lords. There he became skilled in fighting, practising long and hard with weapons and also training in an athletic manner that was unusual for the day. The training included gymnastics in armour and distance running, which must have toughened him considerably. He mixed with the nobility of England and fought for the English king against the French and the Scots. He displayed such bravery and ferocity that he became a legend and had ballads composed about him as 'resplendent in gold and scarlet trappings of the finest kind'; he drove the Scots before him like 'a flock of goats' with nothing but the jagged end of his broken lance. When approaching forty, he retired to his lands at Sycharth, Corwen. The peace and tranquillity that the bards found there was not to last, for in 1400 there was dispute over land between Owain and his marcher lord neighbour, Lord Grey. The situation was clear, Owain was in the right, but Parliament found in Grey's favour declaring, 'what care we for these barefoot Welsh doggies'. Glyndŵr was incensed, but before anything further could be done Grey, anxious no doubt to acquire all the Welshman's lands, betrayed him yet again. The King, raising an army for Scotland, summoned Owain to join it, but entrusted the message to Grey, who did not pass it on, making it appear that Owain had refused the royal call.

Glyndŵr was a proud man. His physical strength and courage were matched by his appearance: he was tall and wore his hair at shoulder length when the fashion was for close cropping. The blows to his pride were intolerable. With several hundred men Owain sacked Rhuthun, Grey's capital, and several smaller towns, but his force was routed by a small English army and scattered. Henry IV marched to Caernarfon,

Owain's lands were confiscated and peace was restored. Henry breathed a sigh of relief and thought it was all over. He was wrong.

In 1401 the Tudurs of Anglesey captured Conwy, a bold action as we shall see when Conwy is reached. The act was seen as a gesture of Welsh defiance against the oppression of England. Owain raised a small army and, as we have seen, against all the odds won a decisive victory at Hyddgen. Sensing a dream coming true, more and more men came over to Owain and the rebellion spread. Owain used guerrilla tactics which were well suited to the terrain, but a large body of his men were caught eventually at Pilleth in the north of old Radnorshire by a large English army. The action was appallingly bloody and ended with the English army fleeing, leaving dead and dying by the hundred. From the earliest days Owain had been touched by savagery, the sackings and firing of towns having been ruthlessly carried out. Here, however, the brutality sank to new depths as recorded by a contemporary Englishman, 'After the batayle ful schamefully the Walsch women cute of mennes membris and pyt hem in here mouthis'. There were no survivors, and the English were required to buy the corpses for burial. It seems that the latent hatred born of years of (effective) slavery was being exorcised in one go. Henry IV was appalled. Owain had requested aid from Scotland and Ireland and, fearful that he might receive it, Henry marched 100,000 men into Wales in late 1402. The terrain and the notorious Welsh weather, together with the guerrilla tactics – Owain's men burnt the crops to stop the English eating them – forced them to retreat. The winter was the worst for years and the bards told that Owain could conjure up this weather for the defeat of his enemies.

Throughout 1403 Owain gained further lands until it was feared he might invade England itself. By 1404 he was so confident and so much in command that he could be openly crowned, and then called a parliament here at Machynlleth. He declared his aims as a separate state of Wales which was to have its own Archbishop at St David's appointed by the Pope; a law system and parliaments based on that of Hywel Dda; and universities to promote Welsh learning and culture. Emissaries were sent to continental Europe and to Scotland, and the French prepared an army for the invasion of England. But when at last Owain was in a good position to defeat Henry, he failed. A French fleet landed at Milford Haven in 1405, the last hostile invasion of Britain, and the combined Welsh and French force marched on England. Eight miles from Worcester Owain stopped. There was no battle, no decisive thrust, only indecision and a slow retreat. The French went home and the tide ebbed quickly. The castles that the rebels had taken, such as Harlech and Aberystwyth, were all retaken; some of Owain's best captains were killed or captured and executed and, by 1412 without having won a decisive battle, Prince Henry had stilled the noise of revolt. By 1415 the country was so quiet that the new king (Henry IV had died in 1413) offered Owain pardon if he would submit. There was no response, and Owain was never heard of again. The rumour was that he retired to his daughter's house near Kentchurch on the banks of the Wye, but there were also strange tales of him living in a cave on the side of Moel Hebog. By 1417 it was said that he was dead.

And what of Wales? It can be argued that Glyndŵr was no more savage than his warlord contemporaries, that his scorched earth policy was necessary to deny the English provisions, that his looting policy was necessary to feed his army. But Wales was ravaged, its dreams of nationhood were again smashed, and its people subdued and shackled as they had been previously. The people of Wales saw Glyndŵr as a man who had promised them everything and very nearly delivered them from subservience. He was, and still is, revered as a supreme patriot. Later, when Tudor kings and queens ruled England and Wales, the magnetism of the man that had led so many so far touched England too. Shakespeare has him thus –

In faith, he is a worthy gentlemen;
Exceedingly well-read, and profited
In strange concealments; valiant as a lion,
And wondrous affable, and as bountiful
As mines of India.

By then, of course, Welsh bowmen had helped the English king to win at Agincourt.

Glyndŵr's coronation and his parliament were held in a building now occupied by the Parliament House in the main street (Maengwyn, Street). The present building is now believed to have been built later than 1400, but it is certainly medieval and one of only eight listed buildings in the old county of Trefaldwyn. Next to the house is a building of the early twentieth century, though it was constructed in Tudor style. The two buildings house the Tourist Information Office and the Owain Glyndŵr Institute, which stages exhibitions during the summer months. To the east of Parliament House, and on the opposite side of Maengwyn Street, is the Court House of the Lords of the Manor that was built, as the inscription notes, by Owen Pugh in 1628. At the other end of Maengwyn Street is the Clock Tower that is such a distinctive feature of the town. The view down the street to the tower from the Court, or Parliament House, is a delight, the wide vista being concentrated by the clock at the far end. The tower was built by the townsfolk themselves to commemorate the coming of age, in 1873, of Viscount Castlereagh, the eldest son of the Marquess of Londonderry who lived at Plas Machynlleth. The tower is 24m (78ft) tall. Plas Machynlleth itself is south of the tower behind an impressive wall, and near an equally impressive array of trees and rhododendron bushes. The Plas is dated 1653, though this is the date of the earliest parts, as the present frontage dates from the mid-nineteenth century. The Plas now houses Celtica, the Celtic interpretation centre that uses the latest technology to present information on Celts.

Going north from the clock, Royal House stands on the corner of Penrallt Street and Garsiwn Lane. This is probably the oldest house in the town as it certainly dates from the fourteenth century and is, therefore, almost certainly older than Parliament House. At the top of Garsiwn Lane there is a fine row of weaver's cottages from 1820, a reminder of the flannel industry that was important to the town for a long period, right through to the latter half of the nineteenth century.

The church of St Peter pre-dates, in parts, the Royal House by about a century, though it has seen considerable rebuilding and renovation. It is certainly true that there was a priest in the town in 1201 as in that year 'Kennig of Machenthleith' witnessed an agreement between the Prince of Powys and the Abbey of Strata Marcella. The present church is very English in appearance, but inside has something of the austerity of a Welsh chapel. Of the Non-conformist chapels the Methodist building in Maengwyn Street is a very pleasant example of the type.

144

Parc Eryri

Machynlleth to Tal-y-llyn

Leaving Machynlleth, the wayfarer follows the main road with great care to Pontarddyfi. It was here that the Dyfi could be forded for the last time before it reached the sea. That was, of course, a contributory factor to the siting of the town, the distance between town and river being a measure of the seasonal flooding of Afon Dyfi. There has been a bridge here since 1533 when a London merchant left £6.13s.4d towards its construction in his will. That bridge, a wooden structure, lasted an amazing one hundred and fifty years. The current bridge was built in 1805, for £250.15s, and is the second stone structure. At this point, Afon Dyfi is still a beautiful sight, wide and placid, but gives little impression of the torrent that carves such a wonderful progress through the land around Mallwyd and Dinas Mawddwy on its way from its birthplace, Creiglyn Dyfi, high on Aran Fawddwy. All ideas on beauty are subjective, but it is likely that the valleys of the Dyfi and the Mawddach, which will be crossed farther north, would be high on everyone's list.

Cross the bridge and go left on the A493 until a lane goes off right (north) at 741019. Follow this lane as it climbs northward. It is notable for the back views to Machynlleth and the Dyfi and its shadiness, the trees being excellent. At the Y-junction, take the left fork. From the gate on the left a few yards up from here, the wayfarer has to reach open hillside at Foel y Geifr (710050). This can be achieved by following the rights of way, that are clearly marked on OS 1:25,000 Outdoor Leisure Map to Snowdonia National Park (Cadair Idris), as going through the forest. This diligent search starts by going across to the forest. (An alternative of going straight on up the path to the forest, and basically northward on forest tracks to the hill seems preferable to all concerned.) From Foel y Geifr, go west and descend to Bryneglwys quarry. The view to Cadair Idris, beyond the Tal-y-llyn valley from here, is quite superb.

Tal-y-llyn

Now the quarry buildings are gone and the mountain is quiet., but in its day the Bryneglwys quarry rivalled Corris, on the other side of Tarren y Gesail. The history of the slate industry is dealt with more fully when the route reaches Blaenau Ffestiniog, to the north, as that town could more accurately claim to be the capital of Welsh slate. Here the slate was of reasonable quality, and quarrying began in 1847. A newly formed company, Aberdyfi Slate, ran into problems in 1869 when the Corris quarries were connected to the Dyfi railway and via it down to a small quay on Afon Dyfi at Derwenlas, and could therefore easily undercut the price of slate from Bryneglwys. The distance between the two quarries was only four miles, but as the journey also included a haul up over the mountain, it was impractical. Bryneglwys had therefore to rely on the original method of shifting slates by packhorse to Aberdyfi. The situation was something that could not be tolerated indefinitely. Either the company built its own access to the sea or it went broke, and so in 1864 the decision was made to build a railway along the valley of Afon Fathew from Abergynolwyn to Tywyn. The decision to build only as far as Tywyn was taken because by then the standard gauge railway had reached as far as Llwyngwril, north of Tywyn. There was a slight hitch in that the connection between Aberdyfi and Machynlleth was to have been made by bridge across the Dyfi estuary from Aberdyfi itself to Ynyslas. This ambitious scheme failed and the line north of the Dyfi was to remain isolated for three years until sense prevailed and it was linked to Machynlleth via a bridge near what is now Dyfi Junction, a little way north of Glandyfi. The quarry company's railway was to be narrow gauge, with re-loading on to the main line's trucks at Tywyn. To connect the quarry to the railway the immense inclines down the bank of Nant Gwernol were built. A combination of winding engine inclines and tramways then joined the quarry to the railway terminus. The trucks on the

146

incline were self-acting, that is the full one going down pulled an empty one back up, but a brake was still required. If the cable broke, or if the cable-to-truck coupling failed, then both wagons fell away towards the incline base. The result was, obviously, disastrous, and some bits of wreckage can still be found in the stream by the patient visitor with a taste for the unusual.

The quarry workings themselves were a combination of mining, as at Llechwedd and Oakeley, Blaenau Ffestiniog, and galleried quarry, as at Penrhyn (Bethesda). In this case the difference was in the seaming of the slate. The 'narrow' vein produced a soft slate, but one which could be cleaved into very thin sheets and which was, therefore, very desirable. Unfortunately the seam was very patchy and the first company bankrupted itself in its efforts to excavate a workable mine. The 'broad' vein was of a very hard and long-lasting slate which did not cleave into a thin sheet, producing instead a relatively heavy slate. The broad seams were excellent, but as there were fewer palaces etc. being built than houses they could not, of themselves, make the quarry pay. The first company wound up in 1883. The new company soldiered on but closed the quarry in 1909. The decision was very sudden – overnight Abergynolwyn becoming a village with no jobs for anyone. A new company opened the quarry again in 1911 and it continued to operate, totally against the odds, until 1947 when it closed again, this time for good. Even at that stage the company had not planned to finish. Close attention had been paid to the site by the Mines Inspector for several years and though conditions were bad, there having been no investment since the 1880s and much of the machinery being of that vintage, the quarry always managed to acquire a little grace. Small rockfalls in the mine chambers had become frequent and then, as if Bryneglwys itself was no longer prepared to live on borrowed time, one day the roof fell in just after the men had departed. To stabilise the whole area, several other chambers were then dynamited. Great care must be taken at the site. Much of it is on private land, and the casual explorer runs a great risk of injury as man-eating shafts and chasms abound, and much of the old building work is in a precarious state.

Below the quarry is the village of Abergynolwyn. There was a hamlet here, little more than the odd couple of cottages, in the days before the quarry, but the village as we see it is a mid-nineteenth-century development, the three main streets, of seventy houses, having been built for quarrymen by the earliest company. As with all Welsh villages there were three chapels, and a church as well. Now, only the Methodist chapel and the church remain in use. The history of the village suggests a more equitable life-style than that followed in the large quarries of North Wales. There was a field that the company rented out, at a farthing per square yard, for allotments. The bakery would bake the villagers' own dough for a penny a loaf, and roast chickens at Christmas. The railway brought in goods from Tywyn, though the village, being below the station level, was served with its own incline. To minimise the inconvenience that this caused, the incline was continued as a tramway behind all the houses to give a to-the-door service. The trucks also took away the contents of filled cess-pits, a most welcome service in a community well separated in time from modern sanitation. The effect of the closure of the quarries was, inevitably, catastrophic. This was especially true of the sudden closure in 1909, though the situation was retrieved when the quarry re-opened within two years. Later closures were more gradual, allowing the villagers to drift away.

It is for the railway that runs from it to Tywyn rather than the quarries, however, that the village is well known. Strangely it is called the Tal-y-llyn railway, despite never having been to, or ever having been projected to go to, Tal-y-llyn. Most authorities believe that it is likely that the English quarry-owners got the name wrong or, more likely, could not be bothered to get it right! In its original form the railway ran from Tywyn King's, named from the owner of the terminal site, to Nant Gwernol, but the

148

train rapidly became a passenger line as well as a slate carrier, the passengers being ferried between Abergynolwyn and Tywyn Pendre, so that the quarry owners could maintain their own terminals, free of passenger encumbrance. On the modern line, King's is called Wharf, which is, effectively, what it originally was as slate was stored and then shipped out on the Cambrian line. The passenger line was opened in 1866 with no intermediate stops, though these followed shortly. At first, engines were operated out of Abergynolwyn which suited the driver, a villager, well. When the engine-sheds at Pendre were completed, however, he was required to take up and leave the engine there. For the journey to Pendre he was given a gravity trolley which he pushed home with one of the trains. At the end of the day he was marooned in Pendre and faced a long, and uphill, journey home. Not surprisingly he soon tired of this and resigned. His replacement was a Tywyn man who excelled himself by driving the train off the end of the line at King's and on to the Cambrian track – a different gauge and at right angles! He was promptly sacked.

The gauge of the railway was 2ft 3in to standardise with the trucks in use on the quarry incline. Tal-y-llyn was the first of all the Welsh narrow-gauge lines to run a passenger service, and the first that was built to operate with steam engines from commencement. Because the passenger service terminated at a distance from the Cambrian line the company ran a donkey and cart for passengers connecting with it. Part of the duties of the employees was to cut grass near Pendre station to make hay for the winter feed of the donkey. In the last years of the nineteenth century, and the early years of the twentieth, the growth of tourism allowed the railway to survive the fall in slate trade. One trip that brought in the Victorian traveller was the grand tour by the Corris railway from Machynlleth to Corris, then by horse-drawn carriage down to Tal-y-llyn lake and on to Abergynolwyn to catch the narrow gauge down to the standard gauge for Machynlleth. The train carried the Royal Mail and operated a curious service for the earliest members of the hill-walking fraternity by towing them in a slate wagon to Tywyn, assisted by gravity and helped by a brake fitted to the wagon. What they were not told was that it was not downhill all the way and that the uphill sections had to be overcome by pushing. By the thirties, pushing had become part of the daily round of passengers as the railway, track and stock, was wearing out. Neither slate nor passengers ever paid well enough for proper investment, and the company rarely had both at once. The line struggled on until 1950 by which time it was the oldest private railway in the world, but then it seemed likely to become another derelict reminder of the area's short-lived industrial past. At that time it was taken over by a group of amateurs who contributed many skills, a quantity of money and, most importantly, enthusiasm and energy in considerable abundance. Now the railway thrives, and rightly so. It travels towards one of the finest valleys in the whole of Wales in Tal-y-llyn, and has a station near the beautiful Dolgoch falls. The trip from Nant Gwernol to Tywyn takes about an hour in either direction and seems an excellent way of re-stocking depleted food supplies, or just idling away a rest day with, perhaps, a few hours relaxation near the sea.

Tal-y-llyn to Cadair Idris

Abergynolwyn lies in the Dysynni valley – which is dominated by Tal-y-llyn lake at its northern end – a valley that is part of a great fault that continues to Bala, sculpted by later glaciation. From the bridge over the river the straightforward route follows the lane north-westward to a cross-roads. Left from here, about 2.5kms (1.5 miles) over Pont Ystumanner, is Craig y Deryn (Bird Rock), one of the strangest features of the Dysynni valley. Here, 6.5kms (4 miles) inland, there is a seabird nesting colony, not of herring gulls that now appear to nest anywhere, but of cormorants. Many, many years ago the sea lapped the foot of Bird Rock and the cormorants are probably a vestigial colony of

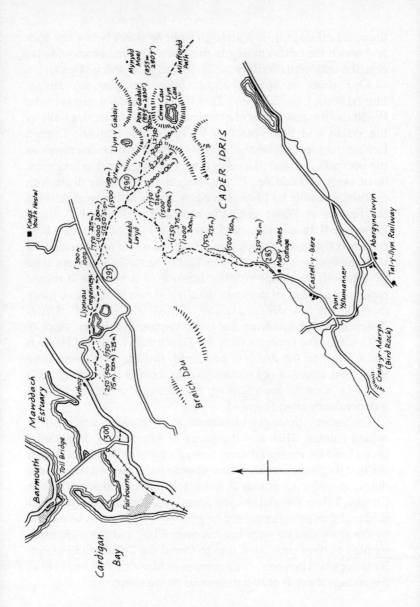

those far-off days. It is a strange sight to stand below the rock and watch the birds circling high above. The visitor should also note the enormous fertility of the lower, guano-rich slopes.

Our route is to the right, however, passing, almost immediately, Castell y Bere. This was one of the greatest of the Welsh castles, making here a distinction between castles built by the Welsh and those built in Wales by the English. Though lacking the sophistication of English castles (such refinements as the portcullis) it was placed in a very strong position and must have been formidable. It was begun in the early thirteenth century, probably by Llywelyn Fawr, and was the royal castle of the Princes of Wales until the conquest of Edward I caused Llywelyn II to abandon it. Llywelyn's brother, Dafydd, then occupied the castle and put up a token show of resistance, until both the brothers were killed in 1282. The castle was destroyed by Edward, no doubt ridding himself of it because it meant more as a symbol of defiance than it did as a stronghold. Since that time it has decayed away, though the general plan is discernible and much of the basic thirteenth-century work is still visible. The contrast with the Edwardian castles of Harlech and Conwy to the north is profound, the site here being little more than a ruin of old stones. In that sense it is a sad site, as it could be seen as representing the struggle of Wales to gain independence from England.

On again, through Llanfihangel-y-Pennant, we reach a ruined cottage. This was the home of Mary Jones, a girl who saved hard for enough money to buy a Bible in Welsh and when she had the money trekked bare-foot to Bala, a round trip of fifty miles, in order to obtain it from the minister there, Thomas Charles. When she arrived she found that the last one had been sold and that no more would be printed. Charles was so moved by the story that he gave her his own Bible, and the incident is reputed to have prompted him to found the British and Foreign Bible Society. The society still possesses Mary's Bible, but here at the cottage there is only a memorial to the event.

From the cottage our route follows the pony track up the valley of the Cadair stream and then up to the col between Cyfrwy and Carnedd Lwyd. Now take the Cyfrwy ridge, a marvellous edge with good views to the northern face of Cadair Idris and Llyn y Gadair, up to the high point of Pen y Gadair.

In choosing this route to the summit the wayfarer has passed some very interesting sites, but he has missed Llyn Cau, arguable the finest lake in Wales, and the entrance to Cwm Cau, one of the most dramatic entrances in Wales. To see these, the wayfarer must follow the B4405 past Tal-y-llyn lake to 730113 where a track leads off north-west. The track starts in wonderful style with a stream to ford and a deeply wooded path to follow, but soon breaks out to open hill with the top of Craig Cau lifting above the ridge ahead. The walker rounds a mound or two and there is Cwm Cau with Llyn Cau nestling at the foot of black cliffs. It is an enchanted spot. To continue to the summit of Pen y Gadair the wayfarer goes south of the lake and takes the obvious track over Craig Cau.

Cadair Idris

Cadair Idris is the first of the truly mountainous regions of Wales to be met by the traveller walking north. It is disappointing that so pure a summit should not reach 3,000ft (915m) and at 892m (2,927ft) Pen y Gadair is lower than Aran Mawddwy, and only just higher than the rounded Pen y Fan in the Brecon Beacons. It is said that those who spend a night alone on Cadair Idris come down either as madmen or poets, a saying that has now become synonymous with the peak. The aphorism is a general Welsh one, however, and was transferred here fairly recently, having been first applied to Maen Du'r Arddu in the Snowdon range. Those who do spend the night here can be comfortable, however, as a substantial hut sits on the top of Pen y Gadair itself. This hut replaces a flimsier one in which a variety of people used to set up a tea shop for visitors many years ago!

The name means chair of Idris though who Idris was is a matter of dispute. He could have been one of the legion of Welsh giants, though the only giant to have actually been connected with the mountain was Gwyn ap Nudd who hunted the hills with hounds for the souls of those who had died on the cliffs. Alternatively, it could be from Idris ap Gwyddno, a seventh-century Meirionnydd prince who fought a decisive battle against the Irish in the area. However, since that battle is occasionally referred to as the slaughter of the Severn, it could have been fought as far away as Pumlumon, which leaves us no closer to the truth.

Any ascent of the mountain is worthwhile, but to see the best that Cadair Idris can offer in terms of scenery the wayfarer should visit Cwm Cau, the finest glacial corrie in Wales, with the steep cliffs of Craig Cau rising above the dark waters of Llyn Cau. The lake, together with Llyn y Gadair to the north, was beautifully described by the bard Gwilym Cowlyd in a Welsh verse known as an *englyn*.

Y llynnau gwyrddion llonydd – a gysgant
    Mewn gwasgod o fynydd,
A thynn heulwen ysblennydd
Ar len y dŵr lun y dydd.

translated as –

The calm green lakes are sleeping in the mountain shadow,
And on the water's canvas bright sunshine paints the picture
of the day.

The cwm is also of interest to the naturalist, the cliffs supporting an arctic-alpine group of plants as well as a fine group of upland birds, including raven and ring ousel.

From the summit of Pen y Gadair traverse Cyfrwy to gain Rhiw Gwredydd (691135), from where a descent northward can be made. Go west, under the crags of Craig-las, to the road at

(678144) where the farm track can be followed, with a continuation to the northern Cregennen lake. This excellent lake can now be reached by a waymarked track from Arthog that can be reversed, following the western side of the stream down to the main road, the A493, at 646146. An alternative is to reach the same point via a minor road from the lakeside, but this misses an excellent piece of walking, though it can be a little crowded in summer as it is a favourite with holidaymakers from Y Bermo. From Arthog, a footpath leads down to the Mawddach estuary and along the railway bridge.

The Mawddach Estuary

Beyond the Mawddach estuary and the spit of land that carries Y Friog (Fairbourne) there was once, in the days before Arthur, a huge sea wall that held back the sea from the fertile stretch of land of Cantref Gwaelod. Sadly the king of the land, Gwyddno Garanhir, entrusted the maintenance of the wall to men who should not have been trusted and it fell into disrepair. Seeing its neglect and a huge storm gathering, Prince Elffin, Gwyddno's son, valiantly warned the people of Cantref Gwaelod. The people made for high ground and were saved, but the wall was breached and Cantref Gwaelod flooded and lost forever. Prince Elffin later found a baby washed up on the salmon weir he had built on the Mawddach. The baby grew up to be the great bard Taliesin, which gave Elffin some joy in compensation for the loss of his beloved land.

To the left as we cross the Mawddach is the small village of Fairbourne which is the unlikely spot for one of the 'Great Little Trains' of Wales. Here a 15 inch-gauge track carries diesel and steam trains along a two-mile track on the sea front. As a ferry crosses the estuary from the track-end to Y Bermo it is worth considering the train/boat method of reaching the town. This would be a highly recommended method of reaching Y Bermo if it was not for the viaduct which is such an extraordinary fine method of doing so, perhaps the best town approach on the route, or in Wales as a whole. The viaduct was built to take the railway into the town in 1860 but, as with several other interesting buildings in Y Bermo, the construction was not without its problems. A particularly violent storm blew most of the structure away at an advanced stage of the first attempt to bridge the river. It is worth remembering if you plan to tramp across it in walking boots with a pack befitting a wayfarer along the spine of Wales, that doubts were recently cast on the bridge's safety, wood-boring marine creatures being thought to have demolished a fair proportion of the underwater piling. Actually the pack would need to be fairly heavy as the doubts were expressed only about the continuing usage of the bridge to carry trains, but more recent tests have suggested that the damage is not as bad as was first feared.

From the centre of the bridge the wayfarer is treated to a fine view of the Mawddach (which vies with the Dyfi for the title of finest river valley in Wales, and comfortably wins the title of finest estuary). Many have spoken of the incomparable beauty of the Mawddach estuary. One Rhys Davies made an acidic judgement on the town at the same time as declaring that the estuary was 'displaying what He can create – in comparison with the work of man in Barmouth'. The description of the estuary is, perhaps, the only truly accurate one that can be offered, and even that does not offer any hope of capturing the essence of its beauty, the play of colours, light on water. Nothing can. The judgement on the town is harsh. In one sense it has truth in that Y Bermo is both seaside town and venerable Welsh port, and suffers from the duplicity, but it is the old port that disclaims the comparison. It may not have the essential beauty of the Mawddach, but it does have a distinct character.

Y Bermo (Barmouth)

The two-edged nature of the town, mentioned above, extends even to its name. The true name is Abermo, itself a diminutive form of Abermawddach, but years of usage allowed a vernacular form Y Bermo to evolve, and this was Anglicised to Barmouth. As a town, its history is very short. It was mentioned in the Merionethshire survey of 1565, instituted by the advisors of Elizabeth I who were concerned at the incidence of piracy in the Irish/Celtic sea. Then it was 'Abermowe, beinge likewise a haven havinge no habitacion. But only foure howses'. The spelling and punctuation are not good, but it is clear that as recently as four hundred years ago the town was an undistinguished place. With the expansion of trading on a countrywide basis, Y Bermo was bound to increase in importance, coastal waters being a safe place for trading boats that could carry relatively large cargoes quickly. Y Bermo's trade and importance, as seen by the number of ships belonging to the port, increased steadily, despite receiving a setback during the Civil War when what then constituted the town was looted and sacked by a detachment of Parliamentarian soldiers. By the end of the eighteenth century, Y Bermo was established as the primary port of Meirionnydd, winning out over Aberdyfi because of the ship-building and repair industries which had sprung up close to the port and along the Mawddach towards Dolgellau.

Much of Y Bermo's trade was in coarse woollen cloth, that was produced in Meirionnydd. Ironically, the cloth was mainly exported to the American colonies where it was used to clothe slaves working on cotton plantations whose product had, itself, killed off large sections of the British woollen industry. Thus, deprived and exploited Welsh workers clothed even more deprived and exploited black slaves who helped their masters impoverish English weavers. The American War of Independence ended the trade at a stroke, and the limited European market was destroyed equally quickly by war with France in the 1790s. Nevertheless the town improved its harbour in 1797 hoping to take advantage of slate, the newest Welsh industry. Because it was not near any of the quarry sites, Y Bermo could not benefit directly, but many of its ships moved slates from Porthmadog and Y Felinheli (Port Dinorwig), and the shipbuilding yards were active building slate traders. Unfortunately, however, the age of the train arrived and with it the decline of the shipbuilding industry, and of the town as a port. Today there are fishermen here, mainly catching lobsters, but in the main the boats are pleasure craft.

Luckily for the town the decline in the port traffic occurred at the same time as the increase in enthusiasm for sea-bathing and seaside holidays. Both of these are relatively recent innovations, despite the idea that the great British holiday seems to have been with us since time immemorial. Royal approval of sea bathing provided the impetus and Y Bermo was equipped with bathing machines by the start of the nineteenth century. These impressive devices were for the use of women so that they should not be seen bathing. Elsewhere they were horse-drawn or winched into and out of the sea. Here they were, initially, fixed so that the bather was marooned for considerable periods by the tide. With the bathers, especially after the coming of the railway when they could arrive in far greater numbers, came a boom in building, with inns, hotels and shops, being erected. For the Victorians, Y Bermo was a delight, the list of notables of the time who came being long, and including Charles Darwin as well as the more romantic names that we usually associate with such spots, Tennyson, Wordsworth and Shelley.

It was to the old town that the romantics were drawn, and it is this area that should be visited to feel the character of the old port, and to see the great contrast to the seaside resort below. Below is correct, for the old port is hewn out of a series of rocky steps with alleyways and passage that connect together in a beautiful, haphazard way. Here the old port is seen to perfection, the houses jutting out of the cliff itself, often reached by stone bridges because of the angles. Here lived a Mrs Talbot who helped Y Bermo to a place in history by her friendship with John Ruskin the social reformer. Impressed by his ideas on housing and social welfare, she gave him some old cottages on the Rock to set up a small housing experiment. Ruskin called his community the Guild of St George and it flourished, the tenants paying a fixed rent and thriving on self-help. This latter element was less influenced by Ruskin than by a Frenchman, Auguste Guyard, a friend of Alexander Dumas and Victor Hugo, and a believer in self-sufficiency, an idea that many believe to have been invented only very recently. Guyard sought refuge here when France went to war with Germany and became a great friend of Ruskin, believing in his social theories and, on a more practical note, helping tenants to grow their own vegetables by terracing the land. When he died he was buried on the hillside above his cottage. However, it is not for this attempt to create the perfect society that Mrs. Talbot and Y Bermo have achieved fame, but for the creation of the National Trust. In 1895 Mrs. Talbot helped create the Trust, probably again with Ruskin's ideas in mind, by giving land on Dinas Olau, the first such donation. A plaque notes the gift, and that it is 'to be kept and guarded for the enjoyment of Barmouth for ever'. The initial idea of the Trust was to preserve Britain's coast-line and, therefore, coastal scenery. Mrs. Talbot died in 1917 at the great age of 93. If she were alive today she would be very proud, and with good reason, of the work of the National Trust today. Below her house, Ty'n-y-ffynnon, is a fine memorial inscription in the rock, less to her than to the ideas of the Trust, and composed by another co-founder of it, Canon HD Rawnsley.

St John's Church near the Peak, as Craig y Gigfron is called by some, though modern – the foundation stone being laid by Princess Beatrice in 1889 – has been claimed to be among the best in North Wales. The church is another of the structures that had construction problems. The tower collapsed without warning when construction was almost complete, severely damaging the main body of the church. Above St John's, on the Peak, is another collection of intricate alleyways and pleasant cottages. One group is called Spion Kop, not after Anfield in deference to Liverpudlian holiday-makers, but after the Boer War battle hill, from which the football crowd terracing also gets its name.

Elsewhere there are other interesting buildings including several old inns, but interest of a different kind can be found in the RNLI maritime museum at the harbour, near where the current Barmouth lifeboat is housed. Inside the small building there are models of the various types of lifeboats, as well as mementoes from the history of the service in Y Bermo, which stretches back to 1818. It is an interesting collection, and a fitting tribute to a group of brave volunteers. Above the harbour the herring gulls wheel continuously. This gull is now very abundant due to its habit of feeding on inland rubbish tips, for which it is much maligned. Despite this, its call still seems to epitomise the seaside and on hearing it, thoughts turn to hot days on long sandy beaches. Y Bermo has those as well, but the sea-bather should beware, for the town is reputed to have a sea-monster living just off shore which has been seen for about one hundred years or so, with the best sighting as recently as 1975 when it was spotted by six schoolgirls.

The Rhinogydd

When leaving Y Bermo the wayfarer is spoilt for choice with regard to paths, as there are several that leave the old and steep section of the town. As good as any is the signed path between the houses that stand a little to the western of the end of the Mawddach bridge. This path leads east of Garn (618165) to a road at (622166) and on towards the WT station (625175). From here the obvious northwards path is permissive, but closed every 5 February so that it will never become a public right of way. It heads north to Bwlch y Rhiwgyr (627200), then continues straigth-forwardly, traversing Llawllech to Diffwys (661234) and on to Y Llethr (661258). From Y Llethr northward are the Rhinogydd.

160

The Rhinogydd are the only piece of Cambrian rock traversed by a route that was to have been designated the Cambrian Way. This lump of Cambrian strata sits over the synclinal Ordovician strata, that form Snowdon to the north and Cadair Idris to the south. This geological position gives the range its alternative name of the Harlech Dome, the castle town being set at the western foot of the range. This is Wales at its wildest. It draws you in on the whaleback of Diffwys, gives you a glimpse at Y Llethr, winds itself up on the two Rhinog peaks and then unleashes the wilderness to the north. The Rhinogydd are a superb range, offering uncompromising walking in exchange for glimpses of wild, beautiful country. This country starts at Y Llethr with its view of Llyn Hywel and the steep slabs that slide into it. There is Rhinog Fawr with its curious banded rock strata, and then the jumble of rock and vegetation that comprises the north of the range.

Between the Rhinog peaks, Fawr and Fach, is Bwlch Drws Ardudwy (the Pass of the Gate of Ardudwy). The land of Ardudwy, sandwiched between the peaks and the sea, holds many surprises, not least the legend of the men of Ardudwy, a band of outlaws who rode through the gateway to loot the outside world, returning to their safe lair. They met their end near Llan Ffestiniog, according to a weird story that will be related later. In the land of Ardudwy there are the Carneddau Hengwm, Neolithic burial chambers which have been called the finest such monuments in Wales (and England), and the Gors-y-Gedol and Dyffryn Ardudwy cromlechs, also some of the finest in Wales. These lie west of Pont Sgethin (634235), which is one of the most romantic sites in Wales. Pont Sgethin lies on a right-of-way traverse of the range, the route following the old coaching road from Bwlch y Rhiwgyr to the bridge. Near the bridge you will pass a memorial stone to Janet Haigh, raised by her son. It is a modest, yet striking, tablet and its final phrase 'Courage Traveller' is in keeping with the track's ancient usage and the modern wayfarer facing the Rhinogydd.

Pont Sgethin still carries a route, a green path, but the sudden appearance of a bridge in the middle of nowhere, can startle. North-west are the ruins of an old coaching inn, another tangible, but less enduring, reminder of a coach ex-Harlech, bound for London, hoping to beat the bandits to the Mawddach. And before the coach there were the drovers, who followed the route north to Cwm Nantcol, the first of two fine cwms on the western flank of the Rhinogydd. At the head of Cwm Nantcol is Maes y Garnedd, once the home of Col John Jones, a signatory of Charles I's death warrant. He was hated by the locals who, presumably, were not too sympathetic when Charles II sentenced him to death after the restoration. Samuel Pepys noted one day in his diary that after hanging, drawing and quartering the 'steaming remains' of Jones were towed around London – suggesting that Jones was no more popular in London. Farther down Cwm Nantcol is Salem Chapel, where Curnow Vosper painted his famous picture of the Welsh at prayer. Locals were paid 6d per sitting in 1910, the painting being 'live', and Shani Owen stood as the central figure. In the folds of her shawl many people see the Devil's face and it is not known whether Vosper intended this as a comment on what he saw as the hypocrisy of people like Shani Owen, or whether it was an accident.

A path leads north from Maes y Garnedd to Llyn Gloyw and on into Cwm Bychan, the second of the two fine cwms. Cwm Bychan is famed not only for its unquestioned rugged beauty, a surprising contrast to the harsh beauty of the northern Rhinogydd, but also for the Roman Steps that rise up Bwlch Tyddiad beyond Llyn Bychan. The site is almost certainly not Roman, the spacing of the steps suggesting a packhorse route.

Our route crosses the two Rhinog peaks to reach Bwlch Tyddiad and the top of the Roman Steps. The quickest route is now to descend the Steps to Llyn Bychan, and then to head up to Bwlch Gwilym and on to Clip. The direct route to Clip can also be followed, but it is hard going and there is no saving of

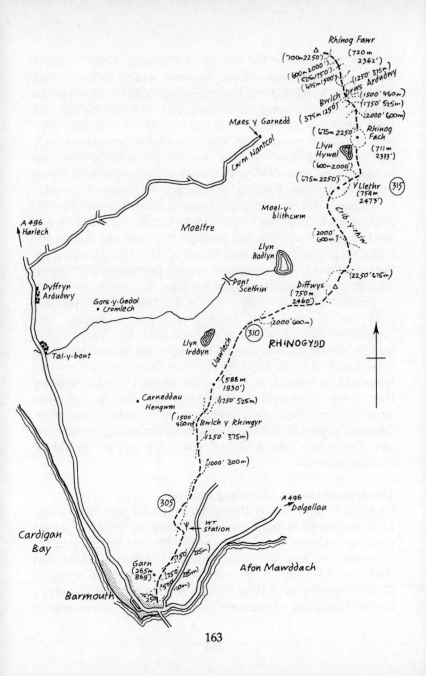

Rhinog Fawr
(700m 2250') △
(600-2000')
(525m 1500')
(475m 1500')
(720 m
2362')

(1250' 375m)
Drws Ardudwy
Bwlch
(1500' 460m)
(1750' 525m)
(375m 1250')
(2000' 600m)
(675m 2250')
Rhinog
Fach
Llyn Hywel
(600-2000')
(711 m
2333')
(675m 2250')
Y Llethr
(754 m
2473')
③⑤

Maes y Garnedd

Cwm Nantcol

Moelfre

Moel-y-
blithcwm

Crib-y-rhiw

A 496
Harlech

Llyn
Bodlyn

(2000'
600m)

(2250' 675m)

Pont
Scethin

Diffwys
(750 m
2460') △

Dyffryn
Ardudwy

Gors-y-Gedol
• Cromlech

Llyn
Irddyn

(2000' 600m)

③①⓪

RHINOGYDD

Tal-y-bont

Llawlech

(588 m
1930')

(1750' 525m)

• Carneddau
Hengwm

(1500'
450m) Bwlch y Rhiwgyr

(1250' 375m)

(1000' 300m)

③⓪⑤

A 496
Dolgellau

WT Station

Cardigan
Bay

Afon Mawddach

Garn
(265m
869')

(750 / 225m)
(750 / 225m)
(500 / 150m)

250m

Barmouth

163

time to compensate for the extra climbing. Now continue northwards over marvellous country, which includes rock pavements, to reach Moel Ysgyfarnogod (659347). North of the peak a footpath crosses the Rhinogydd, following the line of a track which has been used since Bronze Age times. To the north-west of Moel Ysgyfarnogod, the Bryn Cader Faner stone circle lies beside the road. This is one of the most remote and intriguing circles in Wales, its stones set at an angle so that it resembles a crown, a strange (and apparently unique) feature.

To reach this ancient road, head north-east across another peak called Diffwys, and on to Moel y Griafolen, descending to reach a gate at 674358. Go through the gate and follow the indistinct path down to a minor road beside Llyn Trawsfynydd. Turn right and follow the road to reach a footbridge (702349), on the left, over the southern tip of the lake.

Across the lake at every point on the descent to the lakeside road can be seen the Trawsfynydd Power Station. The generating station was nuclear-powered, the only British nuclear station built on an inland site. The reactor buildings were designed by Sir Basil Spence with Dame Sylvia Crowe as landscape architect. It is a matter of personal opinion whether they were successful in blending the site in with the surroundings. The nuclear reactors were of the first generation, 'Magnox' type with natural uranium fuel in a magnesium alloy can. The station closed several years ago and is now being decommissioned.

Trawsfynydd to the Ffestiniog Railway
Cross the bridge and take the road through the grey, slate village of Trawsfynydd to reach the A470 where, at 708361, a signed pathway leads out on to hillside again. The wayfarer now heads northward, occasionally using the masts of the radio station at 709391 as a beacon. To the west, 800m short of the masts, is Castell Tomen-y-Mur. Here stood a Roman fort which, despite the fine views, must have been the last place any Roman soldier

wanted to be posted – the very frontier of the Empire, with pouring rain and 'pagan savages' for company. Interestingly the fort had a small amphitheatre, or possibly a cock-pit, the authorities realising, perhaps, that the lot of the soldier here was not, of itself, a happy one. The fort never saw great service and was abandoned after a comparatively short time. The Normans used the existing fortifications and added a motte, but it was never a popular site and they abandoned it in their turn. Now no stone remains, only the imprint of banks and mounds.

The site has also been suggested as a possibility for the legendary home of Blodeuwedd, the flower maiden, made by the wizards Math and Gwydion for Lleu, nephew of Gwydion, who had been cursed by Arianrhod that he should never have a mortal wife. Blodeuwedd was made out of the flowers and the blossoms of oak, broom and meadowsweet, for constancy, beauty and gentleness. But Blodeuwedd, while beautiful, was neither gentle nor constant, and fell in love with another, Gronw Pebr, lord of Penllyn. She and her lover decided to kill Lleu, which was no straightforward matter as he could not be killed inside or outside a house, on horseback or on foot. They overcame the problems by killing him with a poisoned spear as he swam in the nearby Cynfal stream. At the moment of death he became an eagle which flew away to the gods to be healed. Restored to health he came back to kill Blodeuwedd's lover. She escaped and fled with her hand-maidens, but they were so afraid of being pursued that they walked backwards, and all perished when they fell into Llyn y Morynion (the Lake of the Maidens) near Llan Ffestiniog. Blodeuwedd alone survived and was turned into an owl so that her face would never be seen by day again. This also explains why other birds mob the owl. As we shall see later, however, the lake's name has another derivation.

Our route goes west of the radio station to Sychnant Farm, along the west edge of the wood, and down to the A470 (705404). Immediately opposite a path goes down to Cynfal

Fawr. This is a small manor house with a seventeenth-century front, but later windows. The core of the house is earlier and includes two cruck beams. It was the home of Huw Llwyd, a sixteenth-century soldier and bard. Returning from a long campaign in the Low Countries he was not recognised at his home. Thomas Love Peacock records the return this way –

Art thou a Welshman, old soldier, she cried
Many years have I wandered, the stranger replied,
Twixt Danube and Thames many rivers there be
But the bright waves of Cynfal are fairest to me.

The stone plaque on the house commemorates Huw's grandson Morgan, Puritan writer and mystic, who wrote *The Three Birds*, a conversation between Cromwell, a Puritan and an Episcopalian in the characters of Eagle, Dove and Raven.

The wayfarer has the chance to assess the bright waves of Cynfal as the path drops down to the stream and a waterfall, before climbing again to emerge in Llan Ffestiniog. This is the original village, the slate industry creating the newer and bigger Blaenau Ffestiniog a couple of kilometres or so farther north. To the east of Llan Ffestiniog is Llyn y Morynion (Lake of Maidens) where Blodeuwedd's maidens (from Tomen-y-Mur?) may have drowned. Alternatively the lake could be named after maidens from Dyffryn Clwyd. These were captured by the men of Ardudwy, who were returning to the Rhinogydd when they were overtaken by the kinsmen of the maidens and killed. The maidens, who had fallen in love with the Ardudwy men, could not bear the thought of a return to Clwyd and so committed mass suicide in the lake.

To continue take the lane next to the Pengwern Arms. At its top, go north-west to the cottage at (697424). Go north again and then follow the path around westward and on to the A496 (691422). Turn right (north) and after 150m go left to a drive and then a path going westward. Afon Goedol is crossed by a

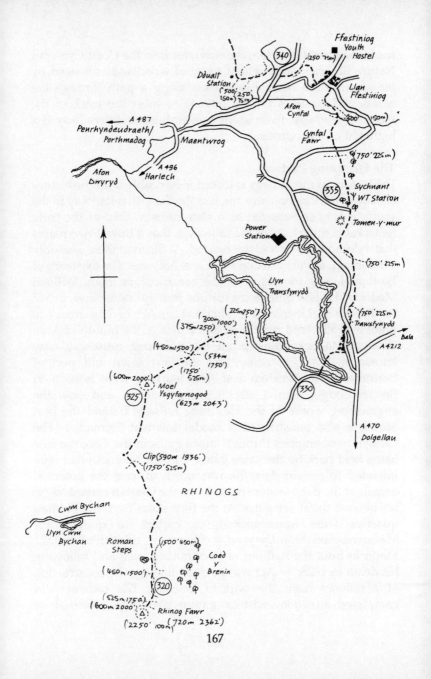

Ffestiniog
Youth
Hostel

(340) (250' 75m)

Dduallt
Station
(500'
150m) (250'
75m)

Afon
Cynfal

Llan
Ffestiniog

← A 487
Penrhyndeudraeth/
Porthmadog

Maentwrog

(300' (50m)

Cynfal
Fawr

(750' 225m)

A 496
Harlech

Sychnant
Y WT Station

(335)

Afon
Dwyryd

Tomen·y·mur

Power
Station

(750' 225m)

Llyn
Trawsfynydd

(225m 750'?)

(750' 225 m)

(300m 1000')

(375m 1250')

(450m 1500')

(534m
1750')

(600m 2000') (1750'
525m)

Trawsfynydd

Bala
A 4212

Moel
Ysgyfarnogod
(623m 2043')

(325)

(330)

A 470
Dolgellau

Clip (590m 1936')
(1750' 525m)

Cwm Bychan

RHINOGS

Llyn Cwm
Bychan

Roman
Steps

(500' 450m)

Coed
y
Brenin

(450m 1500')

(320)

(525m 1750')
(600m 2000')

Rhinog Fawr

(2250' 100m) (720m 2362')

167

footbridge (689424). Here the wayfarer is in the Coed Cymerau Nature Reserve, an excellent piece of woodland enhanced by the stream. The route heads west along a path through the wood, and emerges on the hillside to meet the track of the Ffestiniog railway. Even to the non-enthusiast this railway is a highlight of the journey.

The Ffestiniog Railway

The history of the railway is linked inextricably with the history of slate in the Blaenau area for, like the Tal-y-llyn Railway to the south, it was constructed as a slate railway. One of the truly remarkable things about the railway is that it linked two places that a decade earlier had not existed. At Blaenau there was only a mountain, at Porthmadog there was only sea. The existence of Porthmadog is the result of the work of one man, William Madocks. He had inherited a fortune from his father and, as MP for Boston in Lincolnshire, obtained an Act of Parliament to grant him any land reclaimed in the area at the mouth of Afon Glaslyn. Madocks constructed the mile-long causeway, now known as the Cob, connecting the new town and port of Porthmadog to Penrhyn Isaf. His workers were housed in Boston Lodge, named after his constituency, and now the engineering works of the Ffestiniog railway. Behind the port Madocks also constructed a model town at Tremadog. The Glaslyn now empties through sluice gates in the Cob, the tide being held back by the same gates. Though Madocks had only intended to reclaim land he was quick to note the potential benefit of the deep-water channel that the Glaslyn carved to the sea beyond the sluice gates. At the time slates from the Blaenau quarries were horse-packed, or carted, to quays near Maentwrog on Afon Dwyryd, a dangerous, tidal river. In 1821 Madocks built the harbour of Porthmadog itself and following his death in 1828, an Act was passed allowing the construction of a railway from the port to Blaenau. The railway was completed in 1836, with a gauge variously reported as

1ft 10.75in or 1ft 11.5in. At that time it was for the most part gravity powered, trainloads of trucks falling from Blaenau to Porthmadog complete with a brakeman to prevent disasters, and several horse-boxes to haul the empty trucks back along the 21.5kms (13.5mile) route. The opening of a tunnel through the Moelwyn in 1842 meant a completely gravity powered system. At Blaenau the railway was fed by inclines from the quarries. Since the London and North Western and the Great Western Railway companies also had lines to Blaenau at later stages, and all had different stations, the town is of enormous interest to the railway historian. In general though, it is the Ffestiniog that tourists come to see, and the first thing they notice is that the name is spelt incorrectly, in an Anglicised form with a single 'F'.

The early history of the railway, indeed of all the town's railways, was punctuated with squabbles between them, and with the quarry owners. It appears that the owners were a shrewd lot who had hacked their way upwards and had learnt how to exploit differences and concerns. The biter did occasionally receive a flesh wound however. In 1852 JW Greaves, the owner of Llechwedd Quarry, wrote bitterly to James Spooner, the local supplier of gunpowder, about Spooner's decision to increase the price of powder. 'I think you should have informed me you had raised the price' he states and then – 'When Mr. Curtis was here lately I promised to try his powder'. Greaves enclosed a cheque based on the old price of £40 per ton as opposed to the new one of £42. The plea was ignored, the bluff called and Spooner replied that not only was £40 not enough, but that £42 was now £44, and, more to the point, pay up or else no more powder!

This James Spooner was the son of James Spooner, the first engineer of the railway. Another son, Charles, took over the railway when James senior died in 1856. Charles Spooner's first task was to prepare the track for steam locomotives, a dream of his father's during his last years. It was not only the fulfilment of a dream, however, but business necessity, the horse-drawn system being unable to keep up with the increased tonnages of slate. The problem was that existing designs of narrow-gauge engines would not run on the track, as it was too narrow and too twisty. The solution was a low, square engine of only five tons, the first two being delivered in 1863. Very soon after their arrival the railway opened a passenger service, a description of which offers a beautiful insight into the effect on the neighbourhood of the steam engine – horses galloped, a cow ran over a sow causing much amusement, and the 'amazed specimens of Young Wales' at Blaenau ran from the whistle, not knowing whether to laugh or scream.

The passenger traffic was very important to the railway, particularly when the slate trade declined. To ensure a high standard, the employees were issued with an 86-page volume of regulations including a very long list of fines for misconduct. This included a shilling fine for being on duty improperly dressed, ie. without part of the uniform, or 6d for being untidy. Charles Spooner was a hard man. It is reported that on one occasion when a signalman made a mistake Spooner trekked down to the signal box, hauled the man out and thrashed him with his walking stick. It was not only the employees who had to conform; passengers were requested 'not to lean over, or put their feet outside the carriage, or on the cushions, nor to throw out empty bottles'.

The decline of the slate trade had an adverse effect on the railway's ability to keep up the required level of investment. In the First World War the whole network was taken over as part of a munitions scheme, shells being made at the Boston Lodge works, and this caused a general decline in the condition of the rolling stock. Between the wars a more general decay set in as economy drives were ordered. Winter passenger services were stopped and everything came to a halt in 1939. Following the Second World War the line fell into complete disrepair. Boston Lodge, the engines and the stations were vandalised and looted; grass and trees grew over the abandoned track. Finally, as at Tal-y-llyn, rescue came in the form of an enthusiastic preservation society in 1954. Sadly this was too late to prevent a major disruption of the line, with the dismantling and then flooding of the line around Tanygrisiau, by the construction of the lower reservoir of a pumped-storage power station being built by the then nationalised CEGB. The new society went forward on two fronts, to re-open the line from Porthmadog to Y Dduallt, a halt in the middle of one of the most beautiful of nowheres, and litigation with the CEGB over compensation for the flooded section. The first was a major success, but the second turned into a long and occasionally bitter campaign ending with the society obtaining substantial, but by then inadequate, compensation. As a result, only comparatively recently has the section of track from Y Dduallt to Blaenau been re-opened. That it exists at all is a monument to the amazing energy and tenacity of a remarkable group of railway enthusiasts.

Our route follows the line to the southern tip of the Tanygrisiau reservoir (Llyn Ystradall). The power station on the far lake shore is of novel design, not being a straightforward hydro-electric station, but a pumped-storage station. The major problem with electricity is the inability of the generators or users to store it. Batteries work reasonably well with chemical storage of low voltage, direct current (dc) supplies, but no successful system exists for storing high voltage ac supplies. In a system with many small generating units this is not a problem as, if more power is needed, an extra unit is fired up. With the advent of nuclear power plant, which cannot vary load quickly but is efficient in generating continuous high loads, there was a requirement to store output. Here during quiet hours, usually at night, 'surplus' electricity is used to pump water from the lower reservoir to the upper lake behind the Stwlan dam. Then during periods of high load the water flow is reversed, power being generated as in a normal hydro-electric plant. The power turbine doubles as a water pump. The same principle applies at the bigger station (Dinorwig) near Llanberis.

Also across the water is the town of Blaenau Ffestiniog, not in itself a major tourist town, but close to two major visitor sites for exploring slate mines and the history of the industry.

Slate

The splitting quality of some Welsh rocks, and their use in building, was known very early. Indeed there is evidence that the Romans knew, or were taught, the usefulness of slate, the fort of Segontium outside Caernarfon having been floored, and perhaps roofed, with Cambrian slate. Since the slate must have been brought at least five miles to the site it is inconceivable that the builders used it in preference to locally available rocks for any reason other than its usefulness. Following that usage, that is up to the second century AD, there is an absence of evidence of slate usage until it was recorded that Edward I stayed in a house in the Nantlle valley that was roofed in slate. It is unlikely that these slates were as thin, or as neat, as those of today. Later, when Conwy castle was constructed, the main hall was given a slated roof by Henry le Sclatiere.

Slate beds are produced by compressive forces during earth movements. Because of the localised nature of the compressions the beds were themselves localised. There were five main areas – around Elidir Fawr at the northern end of the Glyderau range, where the Cambrian beds were exploited in the Dinorwig quarries at Llanberis and the Penrhyn quarries at Bethesda; the Ordovician beds around Blaenau Ffestiniog; the Ordovician and Silurians beds around Corris to the north of Machynlleth; the Silurian beds between Corwen and Llangollen; and the Ordovician beds at Preseli in old Pembrokeshire (Penfro). In addition to differences in the age of the rock comprising the slate bed, there is also a considerable variation in colour, although it is sometimes necessary to see two slates of differing colour side by side to be able to distinguish between them accurately. Colour differences also occur within a quarry, the Dinorwig rock having green, red and blue veins, each further subdivided by the colour texture or line pattern, so that there could be a silky, mottled, striped, spotted, curly or hard colour vein. Other areas were similar, though the Ffestiniog slates are almost exclusively of a solid blue-grey colour.

The first development of the slate on a highly commercial basis was at the Penrhyn quarry near Bethesda. The site was owned by Richard Pennant, from the same family as the naturalist Thomas Pennant, who became the first Lord Penrhyn. The Penrhyn family built the huge and luxurious Penrhyn Castle to the east of Bangor. The luxury of the family's lifestyle and that of the Assheton Smiths, owners of the Dinorwig quarry, at Faenol Hall, contrasted fiercely with the conditions in which the quarrymen lived and raised their families. It was said by the latter that if you stole a sheep from the mountain you were hanged, but that if you stole the mountain itself they made you a lord.

Development of the slate at Ffestiniog followed a little behind the workings at Dinorwig and Penrhyn, slate at first being worked only by locals for their own use. This was chiefly because of the difficulty of removing slates from the town. There was a small quay on Afon Dwyryd to the west of Maentwrog, but the journey from the quarries to the quay was 'both tedious and expensive, (the quarrymen) not being, as yet, possessed of a railway, they employ for this purpose about thirty carts, which certainly do not improve this public road'. The latter was almost certainly the case, the narrow-wheeled carts heavily laden with slates churning the roads to such an extent that at one time the Dinorwig quarry owners were forced to use only broad-wheeled carts. The slates to be found at Ffestiniog were of a superb quality, but in addition to the transport problems there was also a working problem, the beds being at an awkward angle and hidden between bands of useless, but hard, rock. The normal open-cast quarrying was therefore at a disadvantage because of the need to remove huge quantities of 'rubbish', as it was actually called, before the slate could be reached. To overcome the problem the Blaenau slate was mined. Even then it was hard, dangerous work. By the early 1900s the annual death rate was 3-4 per 100 with an injury rate of 10 per cent in the quarries and 6 per cent in the mines. One problem was that there was little first aid or rescue service at the sites and injured men were invariably manhandled, which made their injuries worse. Crippled and maimed men were a common sight in the slate towns. Some of the accidents were caused by the unskilled use of gunpowder. This was preferred to any other explosive as it caused a 'gentle' bang; that is the pressures during the blast were small and did not shatter the rock unnecessarily. The powder was loaded into the charge hole which, at first, was laboriously drilled by hand, the 7.5ft (2.3m) hole taking ten hours to drill. The powder was poured in and then tamped down. This itself was an occupation fraught with danger because the tamp rod, or stamper, a rod 76cm (30 inches) long, 6.4cm (2.5in) in diameter, occasionally fired the powder and turned into a projectile which could, and did, kill the operators. The process did offer high entertainment though: in 1902 the Prince and Princess of Wales witnessed a bang at Dinorwig when two tons of powder shifted an estimated 100,000 tons of rock.

After the slate had been removed from the face it was taken to the mill for dressing. The actual splitting has always been done by hand, no machine ever having been invented that could split better than a man. The man sat with the slab of rock leaning against his legs and split it with a broad-bladed chisel and a mallet. In general the slates were split at 6-10 to the inch though in the 1862 London Exhibition the Llechwedd quarries exhibited slates at 16 to the inch, and in 1872 another Llechwedd man split at 18 to the inch. Today, to prove that the craft is not dying everywhere, some splitters can achieve 36 to the inch, though not a roof tile size. After splitting, the tile was trimmed to size. Initially this was also a hand operation, the man marking the slate using a wooden stick with a nail in it, and then giving the tile. a single blow with an iron blade. Trimming machines did achieve some success later. The slates were of standard named sizes, ranging from ladies through countesses to duchesses, the use of exotic names seemingly preferable to 8 x 16 or 14 x 24.

The early working method in the quarries and mines was for a group of men to buy from the management a square yardage of rock face which they would then work to tiles and sell these back to the management. The buy was for a week or sometimes longer, and the agreed price was y *fargian* (the bargain) and was strictly kept. The men bought gunpowder, fuses and, in the Blaenau mines, candles, and hired tools from the owners, and if their bargain was a patch of bad rock then they could work all week and finish up with a loss. It was claimed, by the owners, that the men had to be paid this way; they could not be paid a wage or 'they will do nothing by the day'. Later 'poundage' was introduced to improve matters, this being a guaranteed minimum sum for working so that bad rock bargains did not mean financial losses. A wage system followed, though this was in many instances even worse for the men as the time period the owners had to wait for payment for delivered slate was passed on to the men directly. They sometimes had to go for months without money. In addition, during protracted pay negotiations the owners often refused to pay the going rate, paying instead 'subsist' money that was intended to pressurise the men into an early, and low, settlement. The owners also ran what was sometimes, in these remote areas, the only shop and even, on occasions, paid the workers in tickets that could be exchanged only in the company shop. The poverty in some areas was grim. In 1822 the men of the Nantlle quarry asked for a reduction in the price of gunpowder to that paid at other quarries, as they could no longer obtain credit at the local shop, and had not been paid for twenty-one weeks. Matters could hardly continue in this fashion, and in the last quarter of the nineteenth century the men began to rebel against conditions. The first union was formed at the Glynrhonwy quarry, on Llyn Padarn, in early 1874 and the owners closed the quarry. But at that time the slate trade was excellent – the owners could afford the strike less than the men, who could afford to wait or move elsewhere: within a month the lock-out was at an end and the union established. At Dinorwig the lesson was learned quickly, and within four weeks it too was locked out. Again, this time after five weeks, the owners conceded. In July it was Lord Penrhyn's turn to lock up his quarry. In a bitter exchange of letters between the men's organisers and Penrhyn himself the men pointed out that they were loyal, one of their number having worked in the quarry for more than sixty years, but that they required a living wage. Penrhyn replied that he could not raise wages for three good reasons. First, if he did the quarry would not then give him the profit he required; secondly, the men were extremely ungrateful in not realising how generous he was already; and thirdly, if he did give them more money they would only bring ruin on their families - presumably because they could not handle the cash properly and would get drunk. Not surprisingly the men were very bitter at this and refused to return until Penrhyn accepted the union and increased their wage. After six weeks he capitulated. While Penrhyn's attitude was clearly patronising it is worth remembering that the quarrymen were a hard-drinking and uncompromising breed, a well-known saying being 'I've had a drop too much and its gone to the wife's head'.

Despite the rise of unionism, conditions were still awful by present standards, particularly in the mines of Blaenau Ffestiniog. There the workers lived in houses that were damp, and that had poor drainage and water supplies. Typhoid was endemic and the general overcrowding, together with the high rainfall and inadequate heating, caused a high incidence of TB and pneumonia. The men went to the mine in the rain, worked all day in wet clothes, in wet conditions and with no facilities, and walked home in the rain again. The owners, when challenged by the unions over the conditions, claimed that the men were at fault, as they 'drank too much stewed tea and did

176

not change their underclothes often enough'. This attitude was mirrored in the 1920's when Ellis Davies, the MP for Caernarfon, was fighting for silicosis to be classed as an industrial injury and the Penrhyn quarry doctor maintained that, far from being a hazard, slate dust was beneficial!

At Blaenau Ffestiniog the slate was mined at the Oakeley quarries, owned by WG Oakeley, and at Llechwedd, owned by the Greaves family. Some idea of the effect on the local area can be envisaged from the fact that in 1788 the quarries exported 500 tons of slate, while in 1831 they exported 12,000 tons, a 2,400 per cent rise. In the same period the northern quarries increased by only 450 per cent. Blaenau Ffestiniog's population meanwhile rose from under seven hundred to several thousand. It was 11,000 by 1900, but had fallen to around 6,000 sixty years later. The industry was always a fluctuating one, but by 1900 the trade was in final decline. Llechwedd cut the week to four days in 1905 and then cut wages by 10-15 per cent in 1906 as well as making many men redundant. In 1914 the Blaenau men were exhorted to join up, and their colleagues were put on a three-day week. Men moved from the area to the coal mines of South Wales, and the slate towns became empty. In Bethesda 'shops have now few customers, 1,400 men are away. Misery and privation are present in hundreds of the quarrymen's houses'. In 1971 the Oakeley quarry closed. At the time of closure it was the biggest slate mine in the world, with nearly fifty miles of underground caverns and pathways. In 1972, however, it was re-opened on a reduced scale, together with a museum and visitor centre. On the opposite side of the A470, at this stage rising over the Crimea Pass (Bwlch Gorddinan), is the Llechwedd mine, one of the pioneers of mechanisation of the slate industry. Here electricity was introduced for the first time in 1890, one of its first advantages being to cut the drilling time of powder holes from ten hours to one and a half minutes. Llechwedd never actually closed, though now it too is very much a tourist attraction, including an electric tramway tour through the caverns.

Blaenau Ffestiniog to Croesor

At the reservoir's southern end the route changes to the other side of the railway to reach a footbridge over Nant Ddu: turn left and follow the stream, then maintain direction to climb to Llyn Stwlan, the upper dam of Tanygrisiau power station. From there, bear left (west) to climb to the summit of Moelwyn Mawr, a fine peak offering excellent views in all directions. The peak is descended by the ridge running almost due west – one of the most classical in form in the whole of Wales when viewed from its base at, say, 640446. Continue down to the road and go right into Croesor.

Croesor

It is perhaps naive to write or say that one place typifies an area or a country, particularly in a country such as Wales whose essence is diversity. That said, the first sight of Croesor village does capture, in a single view, something that is North Wales. There, in a valley that is not gentle, particularly in winter, hemmed in by hills which dwarf it in a way that emphasises the smallness of man in the mountains, is a village of a few houses and a chapel. The scar of a quarry can be seen on the hillside, but it has long since closed so that the secluded, private community has ebbed away. This is the land of the holiday home that has brought an untimely end to the Welshness of many villages. There was talk of damming the valley not many years ago and flooding it for a pumped-storage power plant. But despite the attempts to remove it from the map, Croesor lives on. The village received some transient fame in the years around the 1939-45 War because of a remarkable inhabitant, Bob Owen, who was so much a part of the village that he was known as Bob Owen Croesor. Bob was born in 1885 and raised in the village of Llanfrothen, a slightly bigger village than Croesor and about 3kms (2 miles) away. His memory of his upbringing, by his grandmother, would make a chapter in a history of social anthropology. The cottage was one-storey, but the beds were four-posters. Grandmother salted down two pigs annually for food and was an expert with herbs. Bob's schooling (like all his contemporaries and many generations before and after him) was, to his eternal regret, in English and of the English Empire. It had few advantages in a Welsh-speaking community that wished to know the names of Welsh heroes and mountains. His first job was as a farm labourer but his quick brain was noted and he became clerk to the quarry at Croesor. As a farmhand he slept with the other hands in the stable loft. He recalled that snow and rain came through the unfelted slate roof to soak them at night, and that the only drying facility they had was the warmth rising from the horses. He, and many others, suffered rheumatism and arthritis in later years because of this. As clerk to the quarry for thirty years his only memory was of being deputed by the 'absent' manager to tell the men on Saturday that the quarry had closed for good that day and that everyone, himself included, was unemployed. But for all this Bob Owen never gave up his ambition to be a book collector and reader. He collected and read widely, and by the 1930s was a recognised expert on many aspects of Welsh history. In recognition of this expertise he was awarded an honorary MA from the University of Wales in 1931. At that time his library was around 20,000 books, and was of great interest and some value. By the time of his death in 1962, at the age of 77, it had risen to around 50,000 volumes. In the years following the war he became a minor celebrity and had many radio and TV appearances to his credit.

Bob's writings are sparse but are touched with the poetry of the Welsh hills. To read him and of him is to admire him, not in the patronising way that the press of the day referred to him as a self-educated quarryman, but as a man unbound by the apparent brutishness of his early years, completely at one with his life. That last quality is, perhaps, the gift of villages such as Croesor – the way they can offer a glimpse of a truer sense of values.

Also in Croesor is Ffynnon Helen, Helen's Spring. This is named from Helen Luyddog, who may also have given her name to Sarn Helen, Helen's Causeway, the Roman road that traverses Wales from north to south. Helen is reputed to have married the Emperor Magnus Maximus (Macsen Wledig) and persuaded him to build the causeway so that her people could travel more easily. Helen travelled often with her husband's legion, and one day she was on her way from Segontium (Caernarfon) south towards Ffestiniog when she stopped here, where there then was no village but a cool spring. Her party was in two halves, a second group being commanded by her youngest and favourite son. The story is that as her son passed Castell Cidwm to the west of Snowdon the giant Cidwm emerged from his castle and killed him. The truth, if there is any grain of truth in the story at all, is more likely that the boy was killed by his jealous older brother. A courier rushed on to tell the princess the sad news and when told she cried out in despair, 'Croesawr i mi oedd hon' (a cursed hour for me was this). From then on the spring was known as Ffynnon Helen, but the site was called Croesor. This story is just that, and gives no hint of an explanation to the true meaning of Croesor.

The spring is to the right of our route up past the chapel, and that way also is Cnicht, 'the Matterhorn of Wales', a low mountain at only 690m (2,265ft), but of exquisite appearance from this view. Sadly the summit is, in fact, a ridge running away from Croesor so that from all other sides, and the summit, the illusion is destroyed. Interestingly, the elegant name is not Welsh, but English, from the word knight. Leave Croesor along the lane going north-west, and follow this to Bwlchgwernog (612452), reversing the route of the woeful Helen. From here a quiet lane leads to Nanmor, a village whose name, from Nant-y-mor – the stream by the sea – gives a clue to the ancient position of the sea near these land-locked acres. A further clue as to the position of the sea is given in the name of the next highspot on the route – Aberglaslyn.

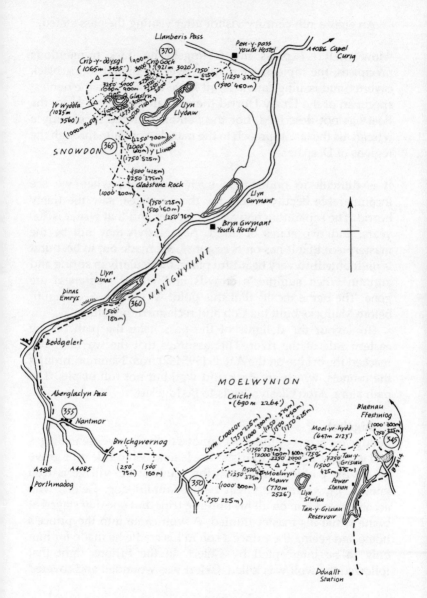

Llanberis Pass

(370)

Pen-y-pass
Youth Hostel

A4086 Capel
Curig

Crib-y-ddysgl   (900m
(1065m 3495') 3000'   Crib Goch
                        (921m 3020')

                                        1750'
                                             (1250' 375m)
            3250' 5000'   2250'   (1500' 460m)
                 1000m 900m   750' 2000'
                      Glaslyn
Yr Wyddfa   475' 1200' 120m
(1035m   Llyn
3560')   Llydaw
            (1000m 3250')

                            (250' 700m)
(365)   (2000'
                             (750' 525m) y Lliwedd
SNOWDON   y Lliwedd

                        (1500' 425m)
                        (250' 375m)
                        Gladstone Rock
                        (1000' 300m)   Llyn
                                             Gwynant
                            (750' 225m)
                             (500' 160m)
                              (250' 76m)
                                  Bryn Gwynant
                                  Youth Hostel

                                              N (compass arrow)

                    Llyn
                    Dinas   NANTGWYNANT

Dinas
Emrys
                (360)
         (500'
          150m)

Beddgelert

Aberglaslyn Pass

(355)   MOELWYNION
  Nantmor
                    Cnicht
          Bwlchgwernog   (690 m 2264')   Blaenau
                                                   Ffestiniog
A498 A4085   Moel-yr-hydd   (1000' 300m)
                   Cwm Croesor (750' 225m) (647m 2123')   (345)
                              (1000' 300m) (250' 375m)   (750' 225m)
Porthmadog   (1250' (1500' 525m)
                                     (1750' 525m)
                                                    175'
                              (1750' 525m)   Moel-y-hydd
                         (250'   (500' (1750' 525m) 600' (1250' Tan-y-
                          75m)   150m) (2000' 900m) 2250' 2000' Grisiau
                                                                  (1500'
                                              175'   425m 375m) Power
                                        (1250' 375m)   Moelwyn   Station
                              (350)   Mawr
                                       (1000' 300m) (770m
                                                     2526')   Llyn
                                        (750' 225m)   Stwlan
                                                         Tan-y-Grisiau
                                                         Reservoir

                                                              Dduallt
                                                              Station

An eighteenth-century visitor after visiting the pass stated,

'How shall I express my feelings! The dark tremendous precipices, the rapid river roaring over disjointed rocks, black caverns, and issuing cataracts; all serve to make this the noblest specimen of the Finely Horrid the eye can possibly behold; the Poet has not described, nor the Painter pictured so gloomy a retreat, 'tis the last approach to the mansion of Pluto through the regions of Despair'.

It is difficult to understand such folly now, when we see incomparable beauty where he, the Classicist, saw the finely horrid. The separation between ourselves and that writer is 200 years, and two states of mind. Aberglaslyn may not be the masterpiece that it has on occasions been made out to be, but it is undoubtedly a very beautiful place, particularly in spring and autumn when summer's crowds and winter's bareness are gone. The name recalls that this point was at the river mouth before Madocks built his Cob and reclaimed the estuary.

To savour the delights of the pass, take the path on the eastern side of the river. This assumes that the wayfarer has reached the bridge on the A4085 (595462) from Nanmor through the tunnels, which are dark and wet, but not full of pits. The path along Afon Glaslyn leads to Beddgelert.

Beddgelert

Beddgelert is one of the most famous of the Snowdonia villages and is a honey-pot for tourists. The legend behind Gelert's grave beside the pathway a little to the south of the village is well known. Llywelyn the Great had a faithful dog, Gelert, who accompanied him on all his hunting trips, but one day stayed at home while his master hunted. A wolf came into the prince's home and seeing the prince's son in his cradle he made for him only to be intercepted by Gelert. In the furious fight that followed the wolf was killed, Gelert was wounded and covered with blood, and the cradle was overturned, the blankets falling on the blood-stained floor. Llywelyn returned and was horrified to be greeted by the bloodied dog. He hurried indoors and seeing the blood-stained blankets and overturned cradle became convince that the dog had killed his son. He instantly drew his word and stabbed the dog whose dying yell woke the baby asleep under the blankets. Only then was the wolf's body found and Llywelyn realised how faithful the dog had been. The remorseful Llywelyn buried the dog with full honours beneath a fine cairn. It is a good story, but it is not how Beddgelert got its name.

The story itself is an ancient one, the first version being in Sanskrit, and even the Welsh version probably pre-dates Llywelyn. It may have been transferred to him because of his own dog, for there is reason to believe that King John gave Llywelyn a deer-hunting dog called Killhart. Beddgelert is possibly named from a holy man, Celert, who lived in a hermit's cell in the area in Norman times. There is also evidence that an Irish chieftain called Celert lived in the area, or at least visited his children who lived here. Then again, there was a group of Celtic monks called Celei who may have had a house in the area. The only certainty is that 'Bedd' means grave. The idea of transferring the legend of Llywelyn's dog Gelert to the area was the brainchild of one David Prichard, the owner of the Royal Goat Hotel whose motive was to increase trade: there is evidence that the old village was called Llan-y-borth, the church of the port, when boats reached Aberglaslyn. It makes little difference now which of the stories behind the naming of Beddgelert is correct; the legend is a good tale, its only sad side-effect being the number of people who only visit the 'grave' and do not recognise the great beauty that is everywhere in the village. As one visitor put it –

Pass on O tender hearted. Dry your eyes.
Not here a greyhound but a landlord lies.

The village is placed strategically at the meeting-point of Afon Glaslyn and Afon Colwyn, and was the site of one of the earliest monasteries in Wales. Indeed it is likely that only the house on the holy island of Enlli pre-dates Beddgelert's Augustinian Priory. In one form or another the house existed from the sixth century, but was endowed by Llywelyn the Great's grandson, Llywelyn the Last, in true medieval fashion in the thirteenth century. In the years that followed it was burnt down, as were so many others, on the odd occasion, but survived until the Dissolution. Nothing now remains, although the church retains some of the original priory church.

Elsewhere the village is idyllic though it can be overpopulated and the old bridge, itself so picturesque, is a nightmare when blocked by holiday coaches. The visitor who wants to see the village properly must be very patient, or must come in winter.

Through the heart of Eryri

To continue, the eastern, later southern, bank of Afon Glaslyn is followed upstream to Llyn Dinas. At 606492 on the northern side of the river is Dinas Emrys (fortress of Ambrosius). The legend connected to this site concerns Gwrtheyrn (Vortigern), leader of the Brythonic/Welsh peoples at some time in the fourth centure, who was greatly blamed for his failure to stop Saxon advances in the Islands. Although the site has Iron Age and early medieval aspects to its true history, it is to legend that we look for the most interesting and significant details. When the Saxons invaded, carrying all before them, Gwrtheyrn asked his magicians what he should do to save himself and they told him to build a tower, which he decided to do here at Dinas Emrys. His masons set to work, but every morning they found that the previous day's work had disappeared into the earth. Desperately, Gwrtheyrn consulted the magicians again, and they told him he must find a boy with no father who should be killed at the spot. When the earth was soaked with his blood the tower could stand. Messengers went far and wide and eventually found (in Caerfyrddin) a boy whose mother was a royal princess who had been made pregnant by an invisible and, therefore, unknown being – an incubus demon, half man, half angel. They took the boy to Gwrtheyrn, but before he could be sacrificed he accused the magicians of false prophecy, claiming that the tower disappeared because of what was under it. Impressed by his manner Gwrtheyrn followed the boy's suggestion, digging into the ground to reveal an underwater pool. The pool was drained and there, as the boy predicted, were two sleeping dragons, one red and one white. The dragons woke and began to fight, the fighting also following prophecies of the boy. First the white dragon was winning, but then the red dragon recovered and beat him away, but just as it was about to kill the white, it started instead to tear itself apart. There were more detailed prophecies, for the boy was Myrddin (Merlin), later magician to King Arthur. This version of the fight of the dragons is believed to be correct, and is thought to parallel the fight between the Welsh (red dragon), and the Saxons (white dragon). In that case it is largely accurate, for the Saxons won until the time of Arthur, then lost badly only to see internal factions in the Brythonic/Welsh camp give the Saxons the upper hand again following Arthur's death. Later writers saw the battle as Welsh against Norman or Englishman and re-wrote the battle scene with the red dragon winning, but Myrddin's prophecy was never actually proven false. The tale itself is fascinating because it ties in with an even earlier one, given in the Mabinogion, of Lludd, King of Britain, who buried dragons at a spot in Eryri to rid Britain of a plague of screaming. Again the dragons were red and white, but in the earlier tale they were found at Rhydychen (Oxford), on the invasion route of the Saxon armies.

Those who would like a closer look at Dinas Emrys can cross the footbridge at 604489, but the fort is on private land. The alternative route is to follow the southern shore of Llyn Dinas on a track heading for the minor road at 627502. The view northward on the path is excellent, with the dark lake and the mountains beyond. That to the south is interesting for those seeing it for the first time, the long ridge to the south-east being Cnicht, which is only Matterhorn-shaped from the Porthmadog side.

The route crosses Afon Glaslyn to emerge on the A498 at 626503. Go right to the start of the Watkin Path at 627506, and follow this northward.

Eryri

Eryri is the Welsh name for Snowdonia, this part of which contains the highest Welsh peak, Yr Wyddfa (Snowdon). The name Eryri is translated as the place of Eagles, which existed in the area until a few centuries ago. In the days of Giraldus Cambrensis they were relatively common. Giraldus states that one remarkable eagle lived in Snowdonia (one bird or one type?), which perched on a particular stone every fifth feast day to be ready to eat the bodies of dead men as it knew that on that day war would break out. He described the stone as having a hole in it, worn by the sharpening of the bird's beak and, to make the story more credible, pointed out that the eagle knew the place it could find its prey, but not the time, while the raven knew the time, but not the place.

Until the latter half of the eighteenth century, ie. before the slate industry, this area was truly wild with no roads and few tracks. As late as the early nineteenth century the original transport system, the horse-drawn sled, could still be seen, towing three-hundredweight loads along the pony tracks. The houses were poor, and conditions primitive as they were in many rural areas elsewhere. The livestock shared the house, cows being at one end and people at the other, with the heating from a central fire below a hole in the roof. In front of the fire there would frequently be a pig happily curled up, oblivious to the sinister significance of sage and onion. Today there is access in plenty and Eryri is reeling under the presence of people. It has things that are irreplaceable, the Snowdon lily, an arctic spider that lives nowhere else, even wild (feral) goats. But mainly it has peace, which is a rare quality. Frequently the peace is shattered by the tourist hordes. The keen or expert walker can always find his peace by moving to a different area, or just moving farther into the hills. But we should all beware. Erosion and pollution are not just a product of the car-borne day tripper, as rubbish in the remoter areas shows. Dr. Johnson, a good few years ago, defined the mountaineer as a 'freebooter or savage'. Today his definition holds good for too many of the breed.

The Watkin Path was presented to the nation for public use by Sir Edward Watkin, the railway magnate, in 1892. To open the path, Watkin persuaded Prime Minister Gladstone down from Caernarfon on 13 September. Gladstone, the Grand Old Man as he was known even then, was eighty-four and in his fourth term as prime minister. It was a vile day with pouring rain, but he and his wife travelled in an open carriage to acknowledge the cheers of the crowd. A great many people then walked, still in rain, to a rostrum where there was hymn singing and speech making. Gladstone spoke on the 'Land Question in Wales' and enjoyed the singing very much, asking for several encores. There were cheers, and the throng departed. Not one word was mentioned about the path which, since the whole thing was staged for its opening, was a little sad. To make amends for this Sir Edward and Lady Watkin, the Gladstones and a few others followed the path the next day. Only Lady Watkin and a friend reached the summit, though many made Bwlch y Saethau. Mrs. Gladstone used a donkey and there were many who wished that the Grand Old Man had used it. This was due to an assault on Gladstone by a cow at Chester a little earlier. After the assault the cow was butchered and sold at a high price, the hide was stuffed and exhibited, and her calf fetched good money. Many felt that if a cow which tried to kill him was worth so much, then a donkey which had helped him might be worth even more!

We follow in the footsteps of those who made it to Bwlch y Saethau and we also see the tremendous view of Glaslyn that opens up. Bwlch y Saethau is the pass of the arrows. This has been suggested as one possibility for the legendary site of King Arthur's last battle when, together with the few knights of the Round Table still loyal to him, he fought against Medrod (Mordred), who had plotted to overthrow him with some renegade knights, and a Saxon army which Medrod had persuaded to help him by offering to divide up Arthur's realm. In that last great battle (at Camlan) the most enduring legend is of Arthur hacking a path through the enemy lines until he came face to face with Medrod. The younger man, struck first and Arthur received a death wound, but Caledfwlch (Excalibur) flashed once more in his hand and Medrod was hit so hard that his helmet was cleaved open, and his head split deep. As hero and villain should, Arthur fell quietly while Medrod fell screaming. The name of Bwlch y Saethau derives from another version of the story, in which Arthur is struck down by a lucky arrow as the Saxon hordes retreated. Either way Arthur lay dying on the pass and was carried by Bedwyr (Sir Bedivere) down to the shores of Llyn Llydaw below Y Lliwedd. There Bedwyr and other knights sat weeping beside the silent body of their King, when Arthur opened his eyes and told Bedwyr to stop crying and to take Caledfwlch and cast it into the lake beyond the ridge. Legend has it that this lake was Llyn Idwal beyond the Glyder ridge which is surely too far, even for a superhero. Bedwyr took the sword, but could not throw it away because of its beauty, and so he hid it and returned to Arthur. The King asked him what he had seen and when Bedwyr replied nothing, he swore at him as a liar and sent him away again. Again Bedwyr hid the sword and returned and again he was reviled, now as a traitor and a liar. A third time Bedwyr went, and this time he threw the sword into the middle of the lake where a hand rose and caught it, waved it three times and disappeared. When told, Arthur was content and lay quietly.

188

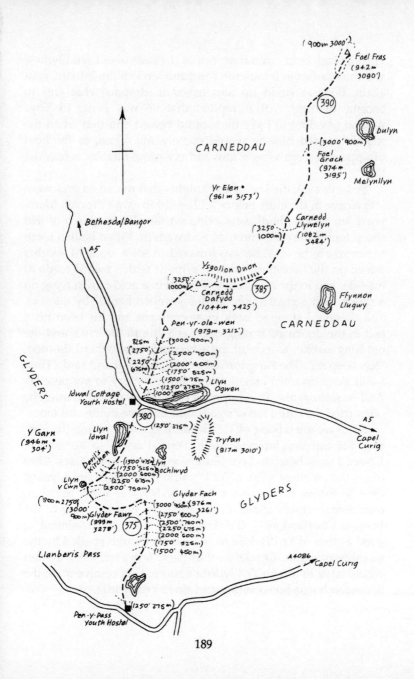

(900m 3000')

△ Foel Fras
(942m
3090')

390

Dulyn

CARNEDDAU

(3000' 900m)

Foel Grach
(974 m
3195')

Melynllyn

Yr Elen •
(961m 3153')

← Bethesda/Bangor

A5

△ Carnedd
Llywelyn
(1062 m
3484')

(3250'
1000m)

Ysgolion Duon

385

(3250'
1000m)

Carnedd
Dafydd
(1044m 3425')

Ffynnon
Llugwy

CARNEDDAU

Pen-yr-ole-wen
(979m 3212')

825m
(2750')
(2250'
675m)

(3000' 900m)

(2500' 760m)

(2000' 600m)

(1750' 525m)

(1500' 475m)

(1250' 375m)

Llyn
Ogwen

1000m

Idwal Cottage Youth Hostel ■

380

(1250' 375m)

A5

Capel Curig

GLYDERS

Y Garn
(946m
304')

Llyn
Idwal

Devil's
Kitchen

Tryfan
(917m 3010')

Llyn
y Cwn

(1500' 475m)

(1750' 525m)Llyn
Bochlwyd

(2000' 600m)

(2250' 675m)

(2500' 750m)

(800m 2750')

(3000'
900m)Glyder Fawr
(999m
3278')

375

Glyder Fach
(976 m
3261')

GLYDERS

(3000' 900m)

(2750' 800m)

(2500' 760m)

(2250' 675m)

(2000' 600m)

(1750' 525m)

(1500' 450m)

Llanberis Pass

A4086

Capel Curig

(1250' 375m)

Pen-y-Pass
Youth Hostel ■

189

Then a black boat came from out of the mist over Llyn Llydaw, and three ladies in it took the King and ferried him into the mist again. Bedwyr stood up and asked in despair what was to become of him? Arthur replied that he was going to Ynys Afallon (Avalon) to have his wound healed and that when the islands needed him he would come again. Then, as the boat disappeared from view a low, sad cry came floating across the lake.

Bedwyr took the last of the knights that remained and went into a cave in the cliffs below Y Lliwedd to await the call. Many years later a shepherd wandering on the cliff in search of lost sheep found the cave entrance and went in. When he lit a torch to see where he was, he was amazed to see a circle of knights asleep on the cave floor, each in armour with a sword ready at his side, and in the middle an old man in a gold crown lying on a couch with a great sword with a jewelled handle by his side. The shepherd stepped back in amazement and his head hit a bell in the doorway. It rang once, echoing in the cave, and the old King awoke. 'Is it time?' he asked and the shepherd shouted, 'No, sleep on'. The King looked at him, nodded and said, 'Then I will sleep on until I shall rise to bring victory to my people'. And he slept again. The shepherd hurried away and, though he often tried, he could never again find the cave in the cliff face.

Since we are talking of Y Lliwedd it is worth noting that one way for our wayfarer to reach Pen-y-Pass is to go over Y Lliwedd from here, and continue along the Miner's Track. That offers the excellent view of Yr Wyddfa from over Llyn Llydaw. One Victorian mountaineer from Wales was once heard to comment during a climb on the Jungfrau that the view to the Bernese Oberland was fine. Indeed, he said, it was almost as good as that of Yr Wyddfa over Llydaw, though spoiled by the quantity of snow. To take in that view, however, the wayfarer would have to forego Yr Wyddfa's summit, so resolve to do the Snowdon horseshoe one day and go to Yr Wyddfa.

Yr Wyddfa

The highest point of the range of mountains, and the highest peak in Wales (and England) is known as Yr Wyddfa. The English call it Snowdon. The cairn at the top reputedly covers the large body of Rhita Gawr, a collector of king's beards who overreached himself in attempting to add Arthur's beard to his collection. Arthur responded by parting the giant's head from his body, resulting in instant death as one would expect, and ordered his men to each place a stone on the dead body, thus creating a cairn. The mountain was thereafter known as Yr Wyddfa, or even Gwyddfa Rhita. Such examples of *onomastic* literature/legends abound in Wales as attempts to give meanings to place names that are a little more interesting than the true explanations. Yr Wyddfa actually means a place with a cairn of stones. One can but sympathise with the creators of the onomastic legends.

Yr Wyddfa can justifiably claim to be the finest mountain in Wales, with its cliffs, ridges and lakes. From almost any angle it is near perfect, but the finest prospect is from the east with the steep cliff of Clogwyn y Garnedd rising above Glaslyn. From the summit on a clear day the visitor may see the Lake District, the hills of southern Scotland and the Wicklow Mountains in Ireland. The ridge walk that links the three 3,000ft (914m) peaks, Y Grib Goch, Crib y Ddysgl and Yr Wyddfa, and continues over Y Lliwedd to make the Snowdon horseshoe, is arguably the finest in the British Isles and must be included in the itinerary of anyone wanting to be considered a mountain walker. From the summit of Yr Wyddfa the wayfarer could take the train, built in only thirteen months in the late 1890s on a gauge of 2ft 7.5in. It is almost 8kms (5 miles) long and for much of its length has a relatively shallow gradient, despite a rack-and-pinion drive. Alternatively the wayfarer must choose one of two routes, either the low-level route following the zig-zag path down to the Pyg track, or down again to the Miners' Track along the lakesides; or take the high level route over the remaining two 3,000ft peaks, descending directly to Pen y Pass from Y Grib Goch. The former is a fine route with excellent views of the Lliwedd cliffs. If Llwybr y Mwynwyr (the Miner's Track) is followed then both the Snowdon lakes are passed. The first lake below Snowdon is Glaslyn, the blue lake, whose more correct, and older, name is Llyn Ffynnon Las, the lake of the blue spring. Here lives one Welsh equivalent of the Loch Ness Monster, yr Afanc, which occasionally – but only very, very occasionally – surfaces to frighten the daylights out of a passing wayfarer. The Afanc lived initially in a pool in Afon Conwy where he made a perpetual nuisance of himself by using his supernatural powers to flood the area when the mood took him, ruining crops and drowning animals. Many had tried to kill him, but his scales could not be pierced by arrows and few had lived to tell the story of their failure. Finally it was decided to use the Afanc's liking for beautiful young girls to lure him to a trap. A brave girl sat on the pool edge and the Afanc, suitably interested, dragged himself out on to the bank and laid his huge and horrible head on her lap. Men appeared from everywhere and the Afanc was chained up, thrashing all the time at the men with his huge clawed feet, and biting at the chains. Two huge oxen were brought from Betws-y-coed and they began to haul the Afanc towards Snowdon. The effort was great, so that at one spot, above Llyn Gwynant, an eye from one of the oxen fell out. The tears shed to cleanse the socket formed Pwll Llygad yr Ych (the Ox's Eye Pool). Eventually, however, Glaslyn was reached and the Afanc was dumped in, the chains having been relaxed. The creature seems to have realised it was beaten because it never used its supernatural powers for revenge, or to move back to Afon Conwy, and in Glaslyn it lives still.

The legend is a very satisfying one, because it shows the link between truth, suitably exaggerated, and myth. At one time there really was an Afanc, but not the crocodile-like creature of the legend, the real one was a beaver. In Welsh the beaver was known as *llostlydan* (the broad-tailed one), but also as *'afanc'*.

The monster idea seems to have been derived from a great flood in the Conwy valley, caused by the breaking of a beaver lodge dam under the weight of winter water. This would also explain the malicious flooding of the area by the Afanc, that appears in the story. At one time the beaver could be found in any of the wooded valleys of Wales, but its fur and meat, and the ease with which it could be killed during its hibernation sleep, meant that it became extinct in the mountain areas of Wales at an early date. By the time of Hywel Dda, in the early tenth century, a beaver pelt was worth fifteen ox hides, suggesting that by then the beaver was scarce. Giraldus tells us, in 1198, that there were no beavers in North Wales, though he maintains that there still were some in Afon Teifi. Clearly the story of the flood in the Conwy valley caused by a water monster became grossly exaggerated in the years following the animal's extinction. It is interesting and, at the same time, sad that such stories should be so readily explained. Of course as late as the nineteenth century a man fishing in the lake attached himself to something that surfaced giving him a glimpse of head and jaws, and he didn't stop running until he reached Beddgelert . . .

Yr Wyddfa to Conwy
All routes reach Pen y Pass at the head of the Llanberis pass where 'A perpetual unbroken Sabbath stillness reigns through the vast profound, except that at intervals. the piercing cry of the kite or the hawk, the hoarse and discordant note of the raven, or the wild minstrelsy of the stream is heard'.

Go down the pass to the east for a few yards for access to the Glyder range which offer some of the most interesting and diverse scenery of any small area in Wales. Between the summits of Glyder Fawr and Glyder Fach is Castell y Gwynt (the Castle of the Winds), a jumble of huge rock slabs which is at the same time both bizarre and yet in no way incongruous. On Glyder Fach the rock slab piles are repeated, here with the added touch of a cantilevered slab which has, to date, lasted the test of time. Charles Kingsley wrote of the summit region – 'that enormous desolation, the dead bones of the eldest born of time', and of the cantilever – 'a line of obelisks like giants crouching side by side'.

From Glyder Fach the *Bristly Ridge* leads down to Bwlch Tryfan which separates the main Glyder mass from Tryfan. The Glyder range stretches northward to Elidir Fawr and Carnedd y Filiast, the former offering views of the lower Llanberis pass, the latter of the beautiful Nant Ffrancon, as the lower valley between the Glyderau and the Carneddau is known. But the interest is drawn towards Tryfan which is a peak for the connoisseur. On its summit there are two standing stones named, for no good reason, Adam and Eve. The stones are, in fact, the top sections of parallel igneous ribs, from which the softer rock has weathered. The truth is mundane; the possibility of a supernatural erection is better, and the freedom of Tryfan offered to those who take the risky step between the two is worth striving for.

As on Snowdon the wayfarer is spoilt for choice with Glyder Fawr, Glyder Fach and Tryfan. As good as any is to climb Glyder Fawr and then descend to the head of Twll Du (the Devil's Kitchen), a cleft in the hillside. To descend, the path must be followed as it goes down the south side (right side from above) of the cleft. The walker is now in Cwm Idwal, the lake of which is the centre of a National Nature Reserve. The plant life of the boggy margin of the lake includes the insectivorous sundew. The lake is also called Idwal, named after the son of Owain Gwynedd, reputedly drowned here by his foster parents.

Continue past the Idwal slabs to the head of Nant Ffrancon. To traverse the Carneddau ahead, the wayfarer must now climb Pen yr Ole Wen, perhaps the steepest walking route in Wales. Cross the Alf Embleton stile (649605), a fine memorial to this treasurer of the Ramblers' Association, discreetly engraved, and start. The climb is about 650m (2,130ft) at about 1 in 2, its only real advantage being that once over it, you stay up for good, the

Carneddau being a series of whaleback ridges all around the same height. The two highest peaks that give the range its name are Carnedd Dafydd and Carnedd Llywelyn, named for Llywelyn ap Gruffudd and his brother Dafydd. Both of these, and Foel Grach and Foel Fras, are crossed naturally in a traverse of the range. Only Yr Elen of the Carneddau 3,000ft peaks is missed, and that can be included if the wayfarer has a will. There are fourteen peaks in Snowdonia over 3,000ft high, three on Yr Wyddfa, five on the Glyderau, and six here. To climb over all of these in 24 hours is a well-known test-piece. The suggested route here covers half of them, and represents a very reasonable attempt for a back-packer.

From Foel Fras, a disappointing peak with a summit trig. point set in a stony plateau much of which seems higher and bounded by a wall that certainly is, the route goes over Drum (709696) and on to Bwlch y Ddeufaen (717717). Even though the Carneddau is losing height now as it falls off towards the sea and the Conwy valley, the interest is maintained with fine views here, and excellent walking north-east to the Sychnant Pass (748770).

Sychnant means dry stream, an accurate description of the valley but hardly one that conveys the elegance of the pass. It is a miniature of the bigger passes, but that helps, the mind being allowed to cope with it at one go. Cross the pass at Pensychnant for the signed path to Conwy mountain. The elegance of form can be seen to perfection from here. It is hardly surprising that Sychnant is depicted on many postcards offering the finest passes in North Wales.

On Conwy Mountain is Castell Caer Seion (759779), which was a Roman fort. The reason for the fort's existence can clearly be seen, the mountain dominating the Conwy estuary and being naturally defended on all sides.

Go east along the ridge towards the town, reaching it at 775778 where a lane leads the wayfarer to his terminal town.

Conwy

As a finishing point to a major walk through, and an investigation of, Wales, there could be few better choices, at sea level, than the town of Conwy. It could be argued that Caernarfon, with its more imposing and symmetrical castle and its royal connections, is a fine end-point, but Caernarfon does not have the charm of Conwy, the little walled town with its castle, river and railway bridges. There was, as we have seen, an Iron Age hill-fort on the mountain above the town, and a fortification existed for centuries on Deganwy mountain on the eastern side of the estuary. Between the two the Romans had an interest here, as the oyster beds at Penarth, on the river a little to the south of the castle, yielded good pearls. Suetonius claims that the chief motive for the Roman invasion of Britain was the pearl fisheries; while this is of dubious veracity, it is certainly true that Julius Caesar had a breast-plate set with pearls from Britain made as a temple gift.

Cistercian monks set up the abbey of Aberconwy on the western river bank in the last quarter of the twelfth century. The abbey was obviously important as it received official recognition of its founding, and a setting out of its boundaries, from Llywelyn Fawr himself. Problems were to follow shortly after, however, as the marcher lords looked covetously at the Welsh lands. Inevitably Afon Conwy became a natural boundary between the westward-pushing Normans and the Welsh, and in 1211 an English army camped on Deganwy mountain. Here they found the remains of the original fort, constructed by Maelgwn Gwynedd, on the conspicuous twin mounds of the mountain top. The river itself proved a formidable obstacle however and the army retreated. In 1245 another attempt was made. This time an English soldier noted: 'there is a small arm of the sea (that) lies between us and Snowdon, where the Welsh quarter themselves, and is, at high tide, about a crossbow-shot wide'. That small distance was sufficient to prevent any massive incursion by the English

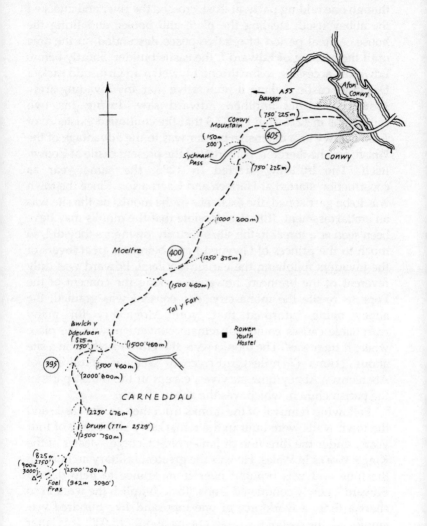

Afon
Conwy

A55
Bangor

Conwy
Mountain

(750' 225 m)

405

Conwy

Sychnant
Pass

(150 m
500')

(750' 225 m)

(1000' 300 m)

Moelfre

400

(1250' 375 m)

(1500' 450 m)

Tal y Fan

Rowen
Youth
Hostel

Bwlch y
Ddeufaen
(525 m
1750')

(1500' 450 m)

395

(1500' 460 m)

(2000' 600 m)

CARNEDDAU

(2250' 675 m)

Drum (771m 2529')
(2500' 780 m)

(825 m
2750')
(900 m
3000')
Foel
Fras (942 m 3090')

(2500' 750 m)

though one raiding party, at least, crossed the river and attacked the abbey itself, stealing the plate and books, and firing the house. A final period of relative peace descended on the area until the coming of Edward I, the castle builder. Shortly before Edward's accession to the throne Llywelyn ap Gruffudd sacked Deganwy castle making it imperative that any invading army should construct another. Edward saw during his two campaigns in 1276-7 and 1282-3 that the continued existence of Afon Conwy as a defensive barrier was to the advantage of the Welsh, and he therefore constructed the present castle at Conwy itself. The building started in 1283, the same year as construction started at Harlech and Caernarfon. Since the town was to be garrisoned, the existence of the monks on the site was an embarrassment. It is also possible that the monks may have been seen as a threat to the site's security, owing, as they did, so much to the princes of Gwynedd and being no great lovers of the invaders following the earlier sacrilege. Edward was duly reverent of the brethren, however, seeking the consent of the Pope to re-site the monastery. The consent was granted, the abbey being informed that 'your Monastery for many reasonable causes could not remain conveniently in the place where it then was'. The monks were therefore resettled on a site about 11kms (7 miles) up-river at Maenan. Nothing of Aberconwy Abbey now survives, except in the oldest parts of the parish church, which was the abbey church.

Following removal of the monks from the site, the castle and the town walls were built in the remarkably short time of four years, under the direction of James of St George, Master of the King's Works in Wales. He was the greatest military architect of the time and was brought over from France to help defend Edward's newly conquered lands. To accomplish the work in so short a time, a workforce of one thousand five hundred was employed, the cost of the project being about £15,000. This latter figure is, in present-day terms, about £7 million, and though such comparisons can be misleading it does give a feel for the size of the undertaking, and the relative cheapness of the labour force who were, in modern terms, being paid about £1,500 per year and finding their own stone out of that. The castle and the town walls were constructed as a single entity, with the castle itself forming the strongest point, positioned in the south-east corner on an outcrop of rock. Before the construction of the two rail bridges which cross the river from the very walls themselves, almost as drawbridges, the castle must have been a formidable sight from across the river. It is of a relatively straightforward design with an inner ward separated from an outer ward by a wall and drawbridge. The concentric design proven at Caerffili twenty years before was not used because of the restricted site. The wards were protected by eight, more or less, symmetrically placed towers. The whole was further strengthened by the presence of east and west barbicans, the eastern one allowing provisioning from a watergate on the river, and the western one connecting with the town by a drawbridge over a moat.

The town walls are about 1.5km (just less than a mile) in length, with three main gates and twenty-one defensive towers, all of which are, to a lesser or greater extent, intact. A walk around the walls is a delightful lap of honour for the successful wayfarer. The three main gates still exist, Porth Uchaf – the upper gate leading out into Gwynedd, towards the castle at Caernarfon; Porth y Felin – the mill gate opening out towards the town's mill on Gyffin Street; and Porth Isaf – the lower gate leading to the beach. As the beach was itself fortified, with the castle at one end and a spur wall and tower at the northern end, this was the way that the majority of provisions arrived. The castle was virtually siege-proof as was proven very early. On his second visit to the castle (his first having been on the way to Caernarfon castle where, in 1284, his son, the first English 'Prince of Wales', was born) in late 1294, Edward I was marooned by the rebellion of Madog ap Llywelyn. As the castle's provisions decreased, the King and his men watched the floodwaters of Afon Conwy which prevented all attempts to resupply the castle from the sea. Thankfully for the beleaguered troops, spring brought good weather and the ships arrived. The record states that the King celebrated a belated Christmas in the castle Great Hall. As part of the 'festivities' a collection of Welsh bards, believed by Edward to have been behind the rebellion, were executed in the town. Only one escaped this summary fate, by leaping from the castle into the river where he was killed instantly.

The wall towers are placed at roughly 50m intervals and are not integral with the wall, there being no continuous walkway from each wall section past a tower to the next section. The gap across the tower throat was normally bridged by planking, which did allow continuous walking. The idea was that the wall itself represented a formidable barrier, but should it be topped the captured section could be isolated from other sections by the removal of the tower planking. The attacker could then continue only by taking the hazardous leap into the town and its waiting defenders. Meanwhile the still-controlled wall sections on each side of the captured section could be used by archers firing at invaders scaling the captured wall. It was a very simple, but highly effective, defence method. At night, and in times of unrest, the planking was left in place, the battlements being continuously patrolled.

Following the siege of Edward I in 1294 the castle had a quiet century, but saw brief action in 1399 when Richard II stayed here on his way from Ireland towards England, and the rebellion of Henry, Duke of Lancaster, later Henry IV. An emissary arrived from Henry to persuade the King to go peaceably to Fflint for a meeting, and was believed when he swore on the Bible in the castle chapel that there was no trickery. Convinced, Richard made off with only a small group of men, but when he reached Colwyn he was ambushed. We learn that 'when he saw the ambushes he was sore abashed, knowing well he was betrayed . . . for he was in such a place as he could not escape'. Richard was indeed captured and, later, was starved to death at the hands of his enemy in Pontefract Castle.

The castle was again in action in 1401, this time on 1st April, which was also Easter Sunday. The commander of the garrison, a John Massey, had taken the soldiers and archers to church leaving a nominal guard on the castle. A band of men led by Rhys and Gwilym ap Tudur, ancestors and members of the family that were later to become the Tudor dynasty, were in full support of Owain Glyndŵr who was at the time in hiding in the mountains of mid Wales. Gwilym ap Tudur gained the castle in a bloodless move, which involved much trickery and good luck, before setting fire to it and much of the town, and in the process destroying many of the records of the castle. There was subsequently a short siege involving the Welsh rebels, and Henry Percy (or Hotspur), who was later to change his allegiance to the cause of Owain Glyndŵr.

Conwy's involvement with the Civil War was strange. A famous son – John Williams, the Archbishop of York, and a convinced Royalist – returned home from York when the Parliamentarian army moved north. Finding the castle in a sorry state of disrepair, he had it restored using money from his own pocket. The restoration was obviously successful, a Parliamentarian army under General Mytton being stopped in the summer of 1646. By that time, however, the Royalist cause was collapsing and there was a lot of bad feeling between the King's supporters. Conwy's governor insulted Williams, who promptly changed sides and joined the siege of his own handiwork. The town fell in August, but the castle held out until November despite a considerable battering that left it ruined. The Parliamentarians treated the Welsh defenders of the castle very honourably, as befitted their bravery, but were less well inclined to a group of equally brave Irishmen who had also helped defend the castle. These were bound in pairs and thrown from the walls into the estuary. Today the outer fabric is complete enough to be wonderfully impressive, although war and nature have taken their toll of the internal work. Of the Great Hall, where Edward I celebrated his belated Christmas over 700 years ago, only a single roof arch remains.

Within the town itself there is nothing of comparable age to the castle – except, of course, for the small part of the church that remains from the abbey, and so pre-dates the castle. It is, however, a delightful place, with rows of tidy cottages, chiefly from the eighteenth and nineteenth centuries. The oldest house is Aberconwy House on the corner of Castle Street and High Street. This dates from the fifteenth century, at roughly the time when Henry VII was founding the Welsh line of kings, the Tudors. It is certainly not a humble cottage, more probably being typical of the style of the town's merchants. With its elaborate entrance and the single overhang it has a distinctly Spanish look. The site is now in the hands of the National Trust and houses an exhibition on Conwy's history as well as a bookshop. Farther up Castle Street is the Black Lion, an elegant, gabled house which has been an inn since the eighteenth century, but was built in the late sixteenth century as the town house of the local vicar. Dating from the same period is Plas Mawr, which lies between High Street and the Terrace Cottages. This is a much grander building, reflecting the increased prosperity of both town and country, and is considered to be the finest Elizabethan town house in North Wales, with much of the carved oak panelling and ceiling plaster being original. The house is open to the public in the summer months. From its upper part there is a fine view of the town. From an architectural point of view, however, perhaps the best building in the town is close to the castle itself, Telford's road bridge. Before its construction the river, which had so effectively formed a barrier to invading armies, was proving an equally formidable barrier to travellers to and from Ireland. During the late eighteenth and early nineteenth centuries the town had prospered from the travellers, with a number of inns springing up to cater for their needs, and a ferry service across the river.

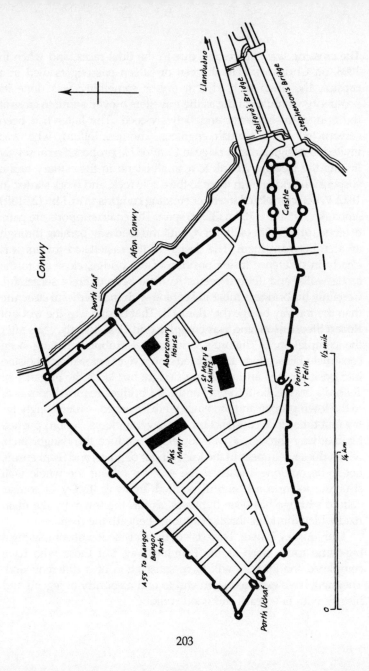

Conwy

Llandudno

Telford's Bridge

Stephenson's Bridge

Castle

Afon Conwy

Porth Isaf

Aberconwy House

St Mary & All Saints

Porth y Felin

Plas Mawr

A55 To Bangor
Bangor Arch

Porth Uchaf

½ mile

¼ km

203

The crossing was dangerous, due to the tidal races, and when in 1806, on Christmas Day, thirteen or fifteen passengers died in a capsize, the town realised that unless something was done its prosperity would dwindle as the travellers moved south to cross at the bridges of Llanrwst and Betws-y-coed. The latter had been constructed by a Scottish engineer, Thomas Telford, who was invited to design a road bridge at Conwy. He proposed a causeway linking the Deganwy bank to a small island in the estuary, and a suspension bridge from there to the castle rock, and work started in 1822. When completed the river crossing comprised a 614m (2,015ft) embankment and a 100m (327ft) span. The chain supports are pairs of stone turrets 13m (42ft) high, with the roadway passing through an arch between them. The design of the castellated towers was clearly in deference to the position of the bridge, close up to the castle walls, and Telford seems to have been entirely successful. Certainly his bridge is more in keeping with the medieval structure than the railway bridge that flanks it. That bridge was the work of Robert Stephenson, and was completed in 1846, twenty years after the completion of Telford's bridge. It is tubular, having been constructed in sections and floated down river before being hoisted into position. It is an interesting design, but lacks the elegance of Telford's bridge. Both the rail and road bridges required entrances to the town proper, and the walls were breached – interestingly for the first time since construction – in several places. Telford pushed his roadway through a wall tower, to produce the Bangor arch, which does not appear in the least bit out of place, and Stephenson, not to be outdone, breached the wall by raising the whole wall structure to form a beautiful pointed archway. Today, of course, Telford's bridge has been bypasses, as has the town, by the main road which thunders through a tunnel beneath the river.

Our journey is over. There is not the satisfaction of completing a big-name route, such as the Pennine Way, but those who have completed the journey will have satisfaction of a different kind. They will have explored from end to end a country of legend and history, with fine peaks and good walking.

Appendix I

The Land of Wales

Wales as a whole is a country of mainly Palaeozoic rocks, Palaeozoic being the name given to a geological era which began about 600 million years ago with the Cambrian period, the earliest period from which fossil remains are commonly preserved. The Cambrian was succeeded by the Ordovician period about 500 million years ago, and then the Silurian period which ended about 400 million years ago, finishing the Lower Palaeozoic. These rocks are the basis of central and north Wales. Indeed, it was here that they were first studied, the names Silurián and Ordovician deriving from tribes of ancient Celts who inhabited parts of the British Isles before and during the Roman occupation.

The Lower Palaeozoic rocks are sediments laid down in a major sea basin, a geosyncline or downfold in the earth's crust, which, in general, subsides as sediment is deposited and precedes the uplift of fold mountains. The downfold had a north-east/south-west trend over central and northern Wales and was formed in the subsiding pre-Cambrian base. Pre-Cambrian is the generic name given to rocks older than those of the Palaeozoic era. In the Ordovician period there was volcanic activity in many parts of north Wales, for instance Cadair Idris and Snowdon; much of the Ordovician rock in those areas is volcanic in origin.

The Lower Palaeozoic deposition was followed, and ended, by an increase in intensity of the 'Caledonian' earth movements that elevated the land mass of north, central and south-west Wales, the sea thus retreating and establishing the sedimentation basins in which the Old Red Sandstone of the Brecon Beacons and surrounding areas in south Wales was deposited. These deposits commenced with rocks of the Devonian period, beginning 400 million years ago. In north Wales the earth movements elevated the area into a huge mountain range. The structure was influenced by the old pre-Cambrian masses of Anglesey and the Bangor/Padarn ridges in the north-west, and the tough Cambrian rocks of the Harlech Dome (Rhinogydd) which acted, to an extent, as resistant barriers against which the softer sedimentary rocks were folded. As always, erosion followed the uplift. The mountains of north Wales were worn down as the limestones of the Carboniferous period, that succeeded the Devonian, were being laid down below a clear, shallow sea at a time when the climate was warm and humid, and the vegetation luxuriant.

Further earth movements followed. The mountains of south Wales were uplifted and folded, while rocks of the Permian, which was the last of the Upper Palaeozoic periods, and the Triassic and Jurassic, of the Mesozoic era, were deposited beneath seas in north-eastern Wales and southern Dyfed. Little is known of the geological history of Wales from this time until the Ice Age of the Pleistocene period, which began only about two million years ago. It may have been under the sea during the Cretaceous period, as was southern England, though no deposits exist to prove this. Perhaps they were eroded away at a later time. However it was during this period – the Tertiary period – that the form we see today was established. The unknown Tertiary period processes produced a gently undulating, dissected plateau (the author suggests that the wayfarer repeats this continuously as he climbs Pen yr Ole Wen!) with apparently little regard for different rock types or their structure. For instance, the river systems have little relationship to their underlying geological structure, and appear to have been superimposed. The courses adapted as different geological structures were encountered due to erosion and uplifts. Such 'pulsed' history shows itself in *'neck-points'* – waterfalls and terraces. The (lower) Clun-gwyn waterfall on Afon Mellte is an example of this rejuvenation of erosion.

As the Tertiary period passed the climate deteriorated, and Arctic conditions eventually came to prevail during the Great

Ice Age. Most of Wales, indeed most of Britain, was covered by a sheet of ice that, at its maximum when even the hills were submerged, was several thousand feet in thickness. The last glaciers retreated only about 10,000 years ago, although truly Arctic conditions had been intermittent towards the end of the age, with occasional periods of plant growth and animal habitation.

Glaciation began with local ice caps on the mountain summits from which glaciers developed to occupy the upland valleys. They then descended to lower ground and merged with others to form continuous ice sheets, known as piedmont ice, which spread over the lowland plains. The existing landforms governed the movements of the glaciers in general, and so the ice utilised the major valleys. From the mountainous centre of Wales there was a radial dispersion, with the ice flowing eastward to the Shropshire-Cheshire plain or the Hereford plain (Severn, Wye, Usk, Dee, Vyrnwy) and westward to Cardigan Bay and St George's Channel (Teifi, Aeron, Ystwyth, Rheidol, Dyfi), as well as southward to the Bristol Channel (Tawe, Neath, Taff, Ebbw) and northward to the Irish Sea. Within this major area were minor centres, where ice accumulated and dispersed. Wales today is much as it was at the end of the Ice Age, and signs of glacial erosion are evident along our route, being a main part of the grandeur of the Welsh mountain scenery. The sources of the glaciers were the amphitheatre-shaped hollows on the mountain sides known generally as cirques or corries, but as *cwm* (pl. *cymoedd*) in Wales. Cwm Cau on the side of Cadair Idris is an excellent example. Many of these hollows have lakes dammed by the moraine of retreating glaciers. Llyn Cau in Cwm Cau is a good example. Associated features are also widespread: arêtes are sharp rock ridges, usually found where cirques erode back to back, a good example being 'Bristly Ridge' on Glyder Fach. There are also screes; the steep slopes of frost-shattered, loose rocks, that are well displayed around Snowdon. There are valleys over-deepened by glacier action giving them a characteristic U-shaped profile with near vertical walls and bevelled spurs, where the ends of ridges that ran into the valley have been worn away as, for instance, on the southern slopes of Glyder Fawr. There are hanging valleys where tributaries entered the over-deepened valleys with, now, a marked change in gradient, such as Afon Dudodyn joining the Llanberis Pass. There are also ribbon lakes occupying rock basins, which are hollows left by the irregular erosion of the valley floor.

As a result of glacial and melt-water erosion, large amounts of rock debris were removed and deposited over the valley floors and coastal plains of Wales. The debris usually comprised stones of varying shapes and sizes, randomly scattered in unstratified clay and sand-boulder clay. More localised deposits, originating from the edges or front of a glacier, are known as lateral and terminal moraine respectively, and these often form a barrier across a valley mouth, or a corrie (cwm), marking the final position of the glacier. Lakes form behind such barriers, a good example being Llyn y Fan Fach, formed behind a cirque barrier.

Apart from the glacial deposits, our route starts in an area with the youngest strata found in Wales – the Trias and Lias of the early Jurassic period covering the Vale of Glamorgan. Northwards, we pass into the eastern part of the South Wales Coalfield, and through towns that developed around the coal, clay and iron ore deposits associated with the Carboniferous rocks of the escarpment – the carboniferous limestone, millstone grit and coal measures. The coal seams and millstone grit are found in cycles and are intermixed with sandstone, indicating a subsidence and subsequent silting up. Because of the cyclical deposition, the millstone grit was known by the coal miners as Farewell Rock, for when it was reached there was little workable coal left on the seam.

Welsh coal may be divided into three main types. The bituminous coals are relatively soft with a high amount of volatile matter making them good house, gas and coking coals.

Anthracites are hard, stony coals with a low amount of volatile matter which burn smokelessly at high temperatures, and are unsuitable for coke. Steam coals are intermediate. The distribution of types is, roughly, governed by the tendency for lower seams at any place to be the most anthracitic, and for a particular seam to become more anthracitic towards the north and west. Thus we have the bituminous coals in the south and east, and the steam coals in the centre.

Another productive portion of the coal measures was the brick clay underlying the coal sea, which represented the muddy beds in which forests of the coal measure had their roots, the coal seam itself, of course, being formed of the compressed, decaying vegetation.

To the north of the coalfield and the limestone outcrops, there is a wide area of gently dipping Old Red Sandstone. Our route takes in the Black Mountains, Brecon Beacons and Mynydd Ddu, the heights of which are part of a steep northern escarpment which runs almost continuously for many miles. The main bulk of the escarpment is formed of resistant brownstones, capped by pebbly plateau beds. The resultant tops are as barren as any country encountered further north. However, in contrast to the north, the relatively fertile red marls of the low-lying areas mean that agriculture is more varied than on the northern moors. The effects of glaciation abound, and are particularly fine in the series of sculpted valleys running north from the Beacons scarp.

Our route moves south of the escarpment of Fforest Fawr, to the 'waterfall' country; an area of millstone grit and carboniferous limestone on the northern edge of the coal measures. The limestone is soluble in rainwater (dilute carbonic acid) and permeable due to the jointed structure of the rock, with horizontal bedding planes and vertical joints. Thus the rock allows water to penetrate and dissolve its way out and, in doing so, to create the features typical of such areas. Where the water disappears underground, the entrance often becomes an enlarged hole known as a 'sink hole' or 'swallet hole'. Commonly whole rivers can disappear underground, leaving a 'dry valley', which adds the erosional effects of the river to the action of the rainwater already underground. Both the Hepste and the Mellte have left dry beds, the latter disappearing at the famous PorthyrOgof (cave). Another typical feature of the soluble and permeable nature of the rock is cave formation, the most famous, but by no means the only, ones being those at Dan yr Ogof.

Rivalling the underground caves and dry valleys in the limestone are the waterfalls and rapids of the Hepste and Mellte. Both rivers have steep profiles, the falls being due to erosion rejuvenation, as mentioned previously, and to fault lines. At Sgwd yr Eira on the Hepste, the most famous fall, a band of shale, softer than the grit above and below it, has been eroded away so that it is possible to walk behind the fall. The fall originated downstream where a fault occurs, and has cut back to its present position. More complex fault movements have taken place at the sites of Sgwd Isaf Clun-gwyn and Sgwd Clun-gwyn on the Mellte.

North of the last sandstone scarp, of Mynydd Ddu, we reach an area rich in mineralisation, as indeed are most of the Welsh Palaeozoic rocks. Lead, zinc, copper and iron ores – commonly these are galena, zinc blende, copper pyrites and haematite respectively – exist as veins, especially in the Silurian rocks of mid-Wales and the Carboniferous rocks of north and south Wales. Once lead was mined very profitably in Cardiganshire (Ceredigion), but it is no longer economic. There are many disused mines on our route, the best being at Cwmystwyth, evidence of Wales's great mineral wealth. The current absence of mining activity has returned the land to its former state. In general the area is a moorland plateau, with rounded hills dissected by river valleys. The moors are often bleak with the soils allowing only sheep farming, and the country becomes more wild and rugged towards and about Pumlumon. This wild, sparsely populated upland with deep winding valleys and numerous tributaries, together with abundant rainfall, has led to the development of the area as reservoir country. The main valleys associated with the reservoirs are those of the Elan and the Claerwen, near Rhayader.

North of the Dyfi, igneous rocks that were occasionally seen as bare crags in mid-Wales are shown in their full glory on Cadair Idris. Igneous rocks are those that have cooled from molten magma, often released during earth movements. Magma which reaches the surface, usually as lava from volcanoes, cools to form rocks known as extrusive igneous rocks, while magma which cools without reaching the surface, and so remains within the rock cover, forms intrusive igneous rocks. Usually in an area where volcanic activity has occurred, both types are found.

The rocks of the Cadair Idris region originated in the extensive, shallow sea in which the Ordovician sediments were deposited. Volcanic islands existed in this area which, when active, periodically spread their products over the normal sediments. Earth movements and subsequent erosion, particularly during the Ice Age, have produced the escarpment we see today.

To the north of the Mawddach estuary is the Harlech Dome, an anticlinal formation of Cambrian sediments bordered by the sea to the west, and a ring of Ordovician volcanic rocks inland. These Cambrian rocks are the oldest that our route traverses, and are hard grits that have produced a wild, mountainous country.

The best examples of the slate industry in Wales are the quarries and mines around Blaenau Ffestiniog, on the north-eastern edge of the Harlech Dome. Slate is one of the products of a third rock classification – metamorphic rocks. These are formed by the action of pressure or temperature on either sedimentary or igneous rocks, producing a rock completely different from the original. In the case of slate, soft shales and mudstones have, under pressure, had their constituent particles both flattened and re-orientated, and are said to adopt a slaty cleavage allowing them to be split in one direction while remaining strong in all others. The process is independent of the age of the rock. In the case of the Blaenau slates, the original rock was lower Ordovician strata. North of Blaenau there are impressive slate workings at Llanberis and Bethesda. Here, however, the eye is drawn, both geologically and scenically, to the mountains around Snowdon.

Northern Snowdonia as a whole is in the form of a north-east/south-west aligned syncline, a complex of minor folds within an overall downfold. There are pre-Cambrian and Cambrian rocks to the north-west, the Cambrian reappearing in the Harlech Dome to the south-east. The region in between is of Ordovician rock, a composite structure with a complicated arrangement of folds and troughs without general trends. The folds are particularly well seen at Cwm Idwal, and below the summit of Snowdon itself.

The landscape we now see has been greatly influenced by glaciation, and excellent examples of its effects abound, one of the best being the valley of Nant Ffrancon between the Glyderau and the Carneddau. This has the typical U-shaped cross-section with many cwms excavated into its sides. The passage of the ice, carrying rock debris, scarred the surface, and an outcrop scoured in this way is often left as an elongated, rounded boulder. Such formations occur often enough to have been named *roches moutonnées*, and a fine example is to be found beneath Tryfan at the head of the Nant Ffrancon pass.

Our route finishes by traversing the Carneddau, the most pastoral, because it is the least igneous-dominated, of the Snowdonian ranges. Its rounded hills, Pen yr Ole Wen notwithstanding, offer a gentle way of reaching Conwy and the sea.

This survey of the geology/geography of Wales is, of course, immediately indicative of the economic history of the country. The fertile coastal plain attracted early settlers, but it was the country's mineral wealth that dominated its economy, with the exploitation of metal ores, coal and slate. Interestingly, the driving force for the exploitation was rarely Welsh in origin. Indeed the social history of the Welsh is one of exploitation by the English. Since our route crosses the South Wales Coalfield, the mining country of mid-Wales, and the slate 'fields' of north Wales, the history of these industries is dealt with in the main body of the book. With the decline of the mineral-based industries, Wales has returned to an agriculturally-based economy supplemented, in certain areas, to a major extent by tourism and the craft industries that spring up around it. Both industries are affected by climate, and the country's weather is very easily summarised. Wales is wet. The upland areas, those taken by the route described, collect a high proportion of the annual rainfall. The Snowdon area receives an annual average of over 400cms (around 160 inches) of rain, most of the upland areas receiving around 250cms (100 inches). To this high rainfall must be added the effect of strong winds, prevailing south-west, and the fact that the proximity of the upland masses to the sea means that the decrease in temperature with altitude is more marked in Wales than is general, at around 0.3°C (0.5°F) per 30m (100ft).

The upland combination of cold, high winds, and rainfall together with generally inadequate drainage have produced a poor soil and a land incapable of sustaining intense and varied plant growth. It is likely that in pre-Roman times the land was deeply forested, but only to about 600m (2,000ft). Above that the moorland was thinly covered with a limited plant life, now limited almost exclusively to grass by sheep grazing, the only economic use in agricultural terms. In the lowlands the rainfall is still high, but the drainage and soil are better, allowing a greater variety of plant life and a more varied agriculture. Those who habitually travel along the high land of Wales may miss this more pleasing aspect of the country, and believe that sparse grass and conifer are all that Wales has to offer. To show that

213

such is not the case, our route has been directed south of the Old Red Sandstone of Fforest Fawr to the limestone country around Ystradfellte, where there is not only some very fine scenery, but the typical flora of carboniferous limestone.

Appendix II

Accommodation

The route described in the book, being unofficial, is not supported by a network of hostels and camp sites such as has arisen around other long-distance footpaths. Indeed, the failure to create an official Cambrian Way led to the demise of the Gerddi Bluog Youth Hostel on the western Rhinogydd. Despite that, the route is well supported by Youth Hostels, at least from the Brecon Beacons National Park northwards, although there are two sections, Ystumtuen to Kings and Kings to Ffestiniog, where detours are required if the walker is not to have long days. However, in each case there is a mid-point town – Machynlleth and Barmouth – where accommodation is obtainable.

Between Cardiff and the Brecon Beacons, the situation is not as good. The loss of the hostel at Crickhowell means that there is now a long day between Capel-y-ffin and Llwyn y Celyn, and the only hostel to the south is at Cardiff itself. However between Cardiff and Abergavenny the route passes through many towns, all of which offer bed and breakfast accommodation, at least.

For the backpacker, the situation is less clear. In Snowdonia camp sites abound and some are in excellent positions – at 739121 below Cadair Idris, and at 672604 below Tryfan, for example – but to the south they are less frequent and less well situated.

Indiscriminate camping cannot be encouraged, and can be easily criticised on the grounds of environmental pollution, not to mention fire risk etc. In the early section of the walk where landowners are more accessible, such camping should not, in any case, be necessary. On balance the backpacker should make every effort to ensure that landowners, conservationists etc. are not agravated by his not stopping wherever he pleases. He should use his tent, with the landowners' permission, until the hostels start and then use these until North Wales is reached where he can safely return to camping.

A list of guest house, B&B and camping possibilities is given in Tony Drake's 'Cambrian Way' handbook, available from the Ramblers Association.

Below is a list of hostels on, or close to, the route:

Cardiff (2 Wedal Road, Roath Park), about 3kms (2 miles) from the start of the route.

Capel-y-ffin (250328) in the Vale of Ewyas north of Abergavenny. About 2kms (1.5 miles) east of the route.

Llwyn y Celyn (973225) on the western flank of the Brecon Beacons, north of the Storey Arms. On the route.

Ystradfellte (925127) about 1.25kms (0.75 miles) south of the village of Ystradfellte. On the route.

Llanddeusant (776245) in the hamlet of Llanddeusant. On the route.

Bryn Poeth Uchaf (796439) east, and above, the village of Rhandirmwyn. About 1.5kms (1 mile) east of the route.

Ty'n-y-Cornel (751534) in the upper Doethïe valley. On the route.

Dôl-goch (806561) in the Tywi valley north of Llyn Brianne. About 5kms (3miles) east of the route.

Blaencaron (713608) in the valley of Afon Groes on the western edge of Elenydd (for an explanation of this area, see the relevant chapter). About 3.25kms (2 miles) west of the route.

Ystumtuen (735786) 1.5kms (1 mile) north of Devil's Bridge. On the route.

Corris (753080) in the village of Corris, north of Machynlleth. About 5 awkward kms (3 awkward miles) east of the route.

Kings (683161) above the Mawddach river north of Cadair Idris. About 2.25kms (1.5 miles) north-east of the route.

Llanbedr (585267) in the village of Llanbedr on the A496 north of Barmouth. About 6kms (3.5miles) west of the route.

Bryn Gwynant (641513) on the edge of Llyn Gwynant. About 1.5kms (1 mile) east of the route.

Pen y Pass (647556) at the head of the Llanberis Pass. On the route.

Idwal Cottage (648603) at the head of the Nant Ffrancon pass. On the route.

Ro-wen (747721) on the eastern slopes of the Carneddau. About 1.5kms (1 mile) south-east of the route.

The positions of the hostels given above, that is 'on' or 'off' the route, should not be taken too literally: as there is no marked route, the hostels cannot be on or off it. The description is meant only as a guide to the position of a hostel relative to the book route.

The list is also not exhaustive in Snowdonia, where slight variations would allow the use of other hostels (such as Capel Curig).

Appendix III

Rights of Way and Access

Those long-distance footpaths in Britain that have been designated by Act of Parliament (the 'official' National Trails) have benefited from the creation, where necessary, of rights of way and the maintenance of paths, so as to ensure that the walker may use them free of any hindrance. The route described in this book has not been designated as official and, in the foreseeable future, is unlikely to be so designated. It is important, therefore, that the walker should be aware of his rights on the route and, equally important, of his obligations also, both to the owner of the land that he crosses and to those who follow him. Though termed a 'right' of way, the walker should also see the pathway as a privilege granted to him by the landowner. He should treat the land with respect, bearing in mind that it is up to him how the next walker will be treated.

A large fraction (more than two-thirds) of the described route is over public rights of way. The right of passage depends upon the type of 'highway' described by that way. On a public footpath the right of passage is on foot. On a bridleway there are additional rights of passage on horseback or cycle. These two rights of way are marked in red on the Ordnance Survey 1:50,000 series maps and in green on the 1:25,000 series maps. Legal orders changing rights of way are usually notified to the OS, but some do not get through, or are not on the current versions of the maps as these are updated at irregular intervals.

In addition to these two types of highway there are also 'roads used as public paths' (RUPPs) which may allow vehicle passage, and 'byways open to all traffic' which certainly do.

Public roads are shown in various colours on the OS maps according to status, but there are many public roads that are uncoloured. These 'white' roads are mostly untarred stony roads or green lanes, and are indistinguishable, on the maps, from private roads. It is, however, usually safe to infer that a white road is public if public paths are shown as terminating on it. The route follows several of these white roads, checks on their status having been made at county offices.

Rights of way have become established by prolonged usage with the acquiescence of the owner of the land, and must be on a defined route. Although many public paths exist over open country, it is common for the way to be less defined. When the survey of rights of way was being conducted from which the definitive maps were derived, uncertainty as to the line of paths across open land often led to their being marked only to the edge of the open country. This was not thought to matter as the facility to roam at large was never disputed. Problems can arise, however, if right of access is disputed. In the law of Wales and England, one cannot establish a right to roam at large by continued usage with acquiescence of the owner, as one can with defined rights of way. The difference between a 'right of way' and a 'right of access' is worth mentioning here. On the former the highway authority has a duty to maintain the highway and to keep it free from obstruction. No such duty applies over the area of land to which the public may have right of access, so that one cannot expect bridges everywhere over streams, or the clearing of gorse and bracken. There are some categories of open country where the public has a legal right of access, and this has considerable relevance to the described route.

1. *Urban Commons*

Under the Law of Property Act 1925, the public acquired a right of access for 'air and exercise' to commons that at the time were administered by borough or urban district councils. At the southern end of the route, this includes Mynydd Machen and a long line of commons from Twmbarlwm near Risca to just south of the Blorenge above Abergavenny. At the northern end, Conwy mountain and the traverse path leading to the Sychnant Pass are on commons in former urban districts.

2. *Crown Commons*

219

Under the same Act, owners of common land were able to make a deed of declaration which gave the public the same rights of access over commons in former rural districts. In 1932 this procedure was adopted by the Crown Commissioners for its extensive commons in the rural districts of Wales (though not for England). Sections of the route run over public-access crown commons, including the northern part of the Carneddau, Pumlumon, the northern Rhinogydd, Moelwyn Mawr, the Teifi pools and the land to the north of these, and around Domen Milwyn.

3. *The Birmingham Clauses*

The route passes over the fringe of the gathering grounds of the Elan Valley reservoirs, which are covered by the famous 'Birmingham Clauses' giving the public 'a privilege at all times to enjoy air, exercise and recreation'.

4. *National Trust Land*

The recent acquisition of part of Snowdon by the Trust has highlighted the organisation's role in guaranteeing access to large tracts of land of outstanding scenic beauty. Several sections of the route traverse Trust land which is open to the public. The longest stretch is the high parts of the Carneddau from the Ogwen valley to Drum, but sections also exist on Sugar Loaf (Mynydd Pen-y-fâl) and Pen y Fan in the Brecon Beacons National Park.

5. *Rural Commons*

Commons in areas administered by rural district councils before 1974 do not normally provide a legal right of access for the public, unless there is a Law of Property Act deed. In practice, the facility to roam is virtually never disputed. In 1986 the Common Land Forum reached a consensus view that there should be a legal right of access to all commons, subject to reasonable restrictions and rules of behaviour, but this was later annulled as a result of grouse shooting interests in Scotland and the north of England.

The longest stretch of rural common on the route is the Black

Mountains section from Bal Mawr via the Twmpa, Waun Fawr and Pen Allt-mawr, to Table Mountain near Crickhowell. All this is very well known as a mountain walk. Other sections are Mynydd Llangynidr and the Black Mountain (Mynydd Du) Common. On these, and all the other commons, there is *de facto* access and no one would dream of trying to contact the owner to ask permission to walk over them.

6. *National Park Authority Land*

Land in the National Parks of England and Wales is generally privately owned, and the National Park status does not give public any better rights of access than on private land elsewhere. However, the Parks have, in some cases, begun to acquire land (chiefly common land) of their own so as to guarantee access. The major areas of interest to the wayfarer are the eastern section of Fforest Fawr and the western side of Mynydd Du. The National Park has also safeguarded access to the western side of Fforest Fawr through an agreement with Welsh Water (Hyder).

7. *Forest Enterprises (formerly the Forestry Commission)*

Forest Enterprises allows general access on foot to its land, subject to certain restrictions.

8. *Countryside Council for Wales*

The Council owns Cadair Idris and Rhinog Fawr and Rhinog Fach, and allows general access.

9. *Tir Cymen Scheme/Tir Gofal*

This scheme (translated as a 'well-crafted landscape') is an experimental scheme under which farmers are paid for managing their land for the benefit of wildlife, archaeology, geology or geography, and for allowing access to it. Under a ten year agreement land near Clip and Moel y Griafolen on the northern Rhinogydd is covered by the scheme. This scheme has now been superseded by a new package called Tir Gofal (since early 1999).

10. *Cardiff*

Cardiff City has no definitive map as yet, but the route follows publicly maintained paths and roads, or is through public parks, or on a council-owned former canal towpath that is open to the public.

11. *General*

There remain a few sections of the route, all on high ground, that do not fall into any of the above categories but which are over open country with de facto access; that is to say that, as far as is known, walkers are not denied access as long as they act in a reasonable manner. The sections are over land which comes within the definition of open country in Part V of the National Parks and Access to the Countryside Act 1949. Amongst the type of country in the definition are mountain and moorland. The Act did not give the public any right of access to open country, but provided the means whereby local authorities could secure public access in cases where it was denied or agreed by the parties to be desirable. A public right of access can be obtained either by agreement, or compulsorily by order. The Act provides for possible limitations on access, such as for periods of grouse shooting, and enables the payment of compensation for allowing access and the provision of a warden service. Although several access agreements have been made in the Peak District, none has so far been made in Wales. It is to be hoped that walkers in Wales will not act in such a manner that access will be denied, precipitating the need to secure access with all the acrimony that would inevitably follow such an action.

Outside all these categories are a very limited number of route sections that follow waymarked routes negotiated by the National Park authorities, including 'courtesy paths' over private land (for instance, the route to the Glyderau from Pen y Pass); unofficial diversions, where the obvious and distinct path does not follow the right of way, though it traverses the same land between the same two points; and paths whose status is uncertain because, while they appear to be in general public use, they are not on the definitive maps and should be claimed at any review.

Index